CRUISE SAVVY

By the Same Author

The Only Way to Cross
Dark Brown is the River
S/S Norway
Olympic/Titanic
*Liners to the Sun
Tribute to a Queen
From Song to Sovereign
Cunard: 150 Glorious Years
Monarch of the Seas
Majesty of the Seas
Safe Return Doubtful
Crossing & Cruising
Legend of the Seas
Under Crown & Anchor
Splendour of the Seas
Grandeur of the Seas
*Titanic Survivor (editor)

*also published by Sheridan House

CRUISE SAVVY

AN INVALUABLE PRIMER FOR FIRST-TIME PASSENGERS

For Elizabeth —
See you on board!
Bless you and
much love from

John Maxtone-Graham

John (& Mary) Maxtone-Graham

S

SHERIDAN HOUSE

First published 2000 by
Sheridan House Inc.
145 Palisade Street
Dobbs Ferry, NY 10522
www.sheridanhouse.com

Library of Congress Cataloging-in-Publication Data
Maxtone-Graham, John
Cruise savvy : an invaluable primer for first-time passengers/
John Maxtone-Graham.
p. cm.
Includes index.
ISBN 1-57409-071-2 (alk. paper)
1. Ocean travel. 2. Cruise ships. I. Title.

G550.M2195 2000
910'2'02—dc21 00-055713

Edited by Janine Simon
Designed by Kirby J. Kiskadden

Printed in the United States of America

Dedicated to those 76 million Americans
whose only port—thus far—is the airport

Acknowledgements

One glaring omission at the back of this volume is a bibliography. It is not there for a very good reason. Few if any published sources exist that would have furnished me with the precise, arcane brew that *Cruise Savvy* demanded. Indeed, had I devised a bibliography, it might well have listed largely my own works, which seems needlessly self-serving. In truth, the raw material for these chapters has been almost totally derived from first-hand experiences and observations aboard dozens of ships sailing all over the world.

Five kind people are due authorial thanks. Eilif Dahl for his information about seasickness, Barry Winiker, ship photographer extraordinaire, whose photographs so enrich the text, Jim Godesman of the Cruise Lines International Association for his invaluable input about Nonpax numbers, my publisher Lothar Simon who came up with the idea, and my dear wife Mary who was kind enough not only to provide one of her stellar indexes but also encouragement, a receptive ear and, always, irrefutable wisdom.

John Maxtone-Graham
New York City, 2000

We drink water from a dipper
You drink champagne from a slipper:
Though it seems
Cruel to bust
All your dreams,
So I must
Here's the truth I tell you...

—Oscar Hammerstein II, *Life Upon the Wicked Stage, Showboat*

Contents

Introduction 1
CHAPTER I: Shipboard—Then, Now, Forever 9
CHAPTER II: Go For It 19
CHAPTER III: But Which Ship and Where To? 28
CHAPTER IV: What to Pack—and Why 38
CHAPTER V: Embark and Explore 59
CHAPTER VI: To Table 76
CHAPTER VII: Evenings 94
CHAPTER VIII: Ashore and Back 109
CHAPTER IX: The Crew, God Bless 'Em 128
CHAPTER X: Delights 152
CHAPTER XI: Horrors 160
CHAPTER XII: Landfall 169
Cruising Glossary 175
Index 179

INTRODUCTION

The one step from the sublime to the ridiculous
is never taken with such alacrity as in a sea voyage.

—Harriet Beecher Stowe, 1853

More than anything else, cruising is passenger. Hull, superstructure, port of call, duty-free shopping, bingo, sunburn and overeating are all secondary; it is the passenger that counts. In-house, that precious human cargo is described in code, a word that crops up repeatedly in cabled messages flashing between ship and shore. The three-letter word is "pax," company shorthand for passengers. It is an abbreviation I shall also use for the purposes of this foreword. Just as Caesar divided Gaul into three parts, so my intention is to divide passengers into three socio/maritime camps.

The first and least numerous are Oldpax, those long familiar with shipboard. These inveterate aficionados started sailing as children and have continued sailing with their children and grandchildren; sometimes they still behave like children.

Oldpax have crossed the Atlantic or Pacific dozens of times and remain dauntingly familiar with global itineraries. They are extremely knowledgeable about ships, the ports they visit and, most of all, how things should be on board. They thrive on good food and service aboard well-run vessels; conversely, if any of the above is amiss, they are not shy about complaining. Among upscale cruise lines in particular, they remain valued if occasionally exasperating clients.

Oldpax know (and are recognized by) a host of captains and crews. Though they will cheerfully invest five-figure sums for an especially appealing voyage, they are still in quest of ticketing or travel bargains. In general, Oldpax remain loyal to one particular cruise line while a select few of my shipboard pals spend their entire sea time aboard one ship only.

The next group is much larger. Newpax are learning the cruising ropes. In search of their ideal ship, they book with a wide variety of cruise lines. Typically, Newpax started their shipboard love affair cautiously, perhaps with a 3-, 4- or 7-day voyage out of Miami, dipping an exploratory toe into the benign Caribbean. Immediately addicted, Newpax subsequently opt for deeper waters, plunging without hesitation into the giddy immersion of a 10-day cruise or, sophisticated passengerhood of a high order, the multiple sea-day bliss of a repositioning crossing across the Atlantic.

Though some neophyte passengers may be gauche and occasionally grating, they are always anxious to learn. Millions of contented Newpax can be found throughout the world's cruising fleet and, each year, their numbers grow relentlessly. When and how do Newpax graduate to Oldpax? I would suggest once they have completed about a dozen cruises and once they are recognized by officers, pursers or maîtres d'hôtel when they embark.

The third and, for the purposes of this volume, most pivotal passenger group are Nonpax. *Nonpax have never booked a cabin.*

(Italics mine.) Though they may be frequent and habitual passengers aboard automobiles, trains or planes, shipboard's inviting gangway remains a perennial unknown. What a paradox—that the world's most comfortable, delightful and seductive conveyances remain bafflingly off-limits for Nonpax.

It is toward this latter and overwhelmingly largest group that *Cruise Savvy* is unerringly targeted. Oldpax and Newpax are invited to enjoy these pages as well but for Nonpax, they are required reading. The Cruise Line International Association—CLIA for short—is a self-governing organization of the world's major cruise players. They reckon that less than five percent of America's eligible cruise passenger pool has ever booked a ship's cabin, that a host of untapped Nonpax are waiting to take the plunge.

Let's talk numbers. Though, on the cusp of the millennium, seven million combined Oldpax and Newpax were cruising, over the next five years, *76,000,000 Nonpax are still out there waiting to be asked!* (More of my incredulous italics.) In other words, for every passenger clambering up a gangway, there are six more potential ones in the hinterlands.

Additionally, there are millions more abroad who, over the past decade, have begun to share America's cruise infatuation. For them, the means are economically at hand. In 1997, a Parisian travel agent friend told me that a family of four could fly from France to Miami both ways and embark on a Caribbean cruise for the same amount of money they might otherwise spend for a week's skiing in the Alps.

Lesson One: Cruising is eminently affordable, far more so than Nonpax realize.

Let me hasten to advise readers turning these initial pages that *Cruise Savvy* is not a guide. There are several well-established volumes on the market, some put together by longtime shipmates of mine: *Fielding's Guide*—edited by Harry Basch and Shirley Slater—as well as Doug Ward's *Berlitz Guide* are two of the most popular. I was once approached by a popular travel publisher who asked me to edit my own cruise ship guide. I declined for one simple but cogent reason. To my mind, cruise guides, however well intentioned, however embellished with persuasive statistics or beguiling prose, attempt the impossible. How can one hope to reduce such a rich, shipboard experience into a few lines of impartial cold type, rating and hence ranking competing cruise lines' products? I am convinced it can not—indeed, *should* not—be done.

I sense that the popularity of cruise ship guides is yet one more manifestation of America's obsession with lists—the best-dressed, the worst-dressed, the ten richest, the ten best cities, the ten best restaurants, the hundred best books—the best everything. But in the matter of cruising, shipboard's complex resonances defy encapsulation within a convenient paragraph or two. One might as well try to rate parenting, ambition, contentment or despair.

Submitting to a personal test case, I think back over past voyages to see if one seems necessarily superior to another. Was it, for example, more desirable to be crossing eastbound on QUEEN ELIZABETH 2 in December of 1997 than traveling up Norway's coast aboard little NORDLYS the summer before? Similarly, can one compare a SEA GODDESS repositioning between Las Palmas and St Croix with the maiden voyage of LEGEND OF THE SEAS from Southampton to Barcelona? How does one equate the novel delights of NORWAY's delivery crossing of 1980 to a 1968 Christmas cruise aboard the same vessel when she was FRANCE? And out here in the Pacific, where these paragraphs are being wrought, how to compare our idyllic southbound plod aboard ISLAND PRINCESS with venerable ROTTERDAM steaming purposefully northwest from Hawaii to Hong Kong in the early eighties? In brief, it cannot be done.

Lesson Two: No two cruises or two cruise ships are either alike or comparable.

Too many variables dictate enjoyment of a ship: the weather, the food, your fellow passengers, table companions, the itinerary, the cabin steward, the entertainment, the multi-faceted crew, your state of health, the onboard mood and, extremely significant, the vessel's architectural design. No contrived formula can be applied to marshal all those disparate factors into one punchy—and reliable—evaluation. The old bromide about "apples and oranges" does not even come close.

Since I am privileged to spend a third of each year afloat lecturing to passengers, I am asked by friends and strangers alike more often than I can count: "What's the best cruise line?" I am always at a loss. By "best," do they mean the most expensive or the least expensive? Do they mean the most lavish, the most select, the most adventurous or the most comfortable? However genuine their query, they ask the impossible. For the appeal of every vessel depends on so many imponderables that, just as I am unable to rate cruises, no more can I rank companies or individual ships. Moreover, I mistrust anyone making such a claim.

This compulsion to poll infects the press as well. I cannot count the number of times interviewers have inquired, almost conspiratorially: "What's your favorite ship?" I always respond, "The one I'm on." And that is not just a tactful copout, I really mean it. The great English stage director Tyrone Guthrie once wrote that, over his theatrical lifetime, he had probably seen at least 50 productions of *Hamlet*, ranging from the West End to Broadway to one of several Stratfords right down to amateur high school performances. And he confessed that, invariably, he had learned something new from every one of them. So too, after seven decades of shipboard, have I gleaned something of interest and value following every embarkation. I can quite honestly say that I have fully enjoyed every one of hundreds of voyages.

Lesson Three : Every sea journey, whether Caribbean circuit, Alaskan excursion or ocean crossing, remains unique.

Nonpax all, come board with me. I am selling neither specific vessel nor itinerary, neither particular cruise line nor destination. *I simply want to turn you on to shipboard*! I want to show you the ropes, prepare you for the delights to come and warn you about pitfalls. For starters, take my word for it: There is nothing else in the vacation world to compare with cruising, nor is there any destination that offers more sybaritic and psychological delight than embarking on a ship bound for sea.

As I was finishing my breakfast this morning, I watched a passenger linger for at least ten minutes at the forward railing atop the bridge. There was nothing to see but ocean. ISLAND PRINCESS was traversing a sunlit Pacific somewhere across those vast, indeterminate sea margins separating the Philippines from Indonesia.

My attention was less on our benign surround than that solitary passenger leaning pensively against the rail. (There is, incidentally, nothing to compare with the comforting support of a varnished teak railing, warm to the touch, exactly the right height and a superb vantage point.) Our breeze of passage ruffled his trousers and shirt as he stood in that bright morning sun, lost in reverie. It occurred to me that, were he to find him-

Lost in reverie, a Royal Viking passenger lingers at the ship's rail. *Author's Collection*

self at that identical stretch of railing once the ship had tied up in San Francisco, he would pass it by without a thought.

Lesson Four: Sea time is magic.

Final Nonpax advisory, you should always remember that *pax* is also the Latin word for peace. Peace is without question the most rewarding dividend of afloat—detachment from the cares infesting the shore, aboard that most serene and blessed conveyance in the world, the cruise ship.

CHAPTER I

SHIPBOARD—THEN, NOW, FOREVER

Old and young, we are all on our last cruise.

—Robert Louis Stevenson, *Crabbed Age and Youth*

It took me five years to talk my wife into a cruise and now I can't keep her off a ship.

—Don Wohlers

This volume should by no means be construed as a purely historical work. Yet, by the same token, we cannot deal with life aboard today's cruise ships without elaborating on yesterday's shipboard. In truth, ever since the first caveman persuaded one of his fellows to join him for a trip in a hollowed-out tree trunk, passengers and the conveyances on which they embark have been congenially paired.

Of course, the beginning of the end for ocean liners occurred on June 29, 1939. That was the day the first scheduled transatlantic aircraft—Boeing's B-314 Dixie Clipper—lofted an historic and adventurous passenger-load from New York's La Guardia Marine Terminal to Lisbon. As though anxious to ease their clients' transition from sea to sky, Pan American embarked them in what they dubbed flying boats. They were advertised as Pan Am Clippers, a name co-opted from reassuringly fast, nineteenth-century cargo vessels. Whereas Lindbergh and Corrigan pioneered transatlantic crossings by air, it was Pan American's clipper service of 1939 that first made them available to the public.

It fascinates me, incidentally, how aircraft terminology remains nostalgically linked to the vessels they supplanted. We "board" modern-day jets, having committed our luggage to the "hold," we are accommodated within a passenger "cabin" behind "pilots" who occupy "cockpits" on the flight "deck;" once land-based "tugs" have pushed back the aircraft, a "purser" attends to our airborne needs; and in the event of turbulence, our aircraft may well "pitch, roll or yaw." One of Britain's Imperial flying boats even came equipped with a 12-foot promenade deck.

Prior to the airborne alternative, the only way to go abroad was by sea. Indeed, that unavoidable ocean passage served as a great leveler. Traveling east or west beyond the continental United States, everyone—whether plutocrat or peon, industrialist or immigrant, statesman or stevedore—was obliged to embark aboard an ocean liner.

They were called ocean liners quite simply because they completed line voyages, sailing from point A to point B—from New York to Southampton, Le Havre, Rotterdam or Hamburg as well as the reverse, their departures and arrivals adhering to a fixed schedule.

In addition to passengers, liners loaded cargo as well, the most important component of which were stout canvas sacks of international mail. Prior to 1939, all transatlantic letters and parcels were dispatched aboard ocean liners. Hence, Britain's honorific maritime prefix "RMS" which stood for Royal Mail Ship; this signified that Cunard's RMS AQUITANIA, for example, had been awarded His or Her Majesty's mail contract.

Long before the PanAm Clippers, there were some novel attempts at speeding select shipboard post by air. Several steamers, including LEVIATHAN, ILE DE FRANCE and, most professional of all, BREMEN, launched airplanes while at sea hundreds of miles away from New York. A few sacks of primitive "air mail" were flown ashore for swifter delivery. Having completed its flight from out in the Atlantic, BREMEN's seaplane used to taxi up to Manhattan's North German Lloyd pier a full day before its parent vessel steamed up-harbor. However, those flights were largely experimental, little more than publicity gimmicks that could only hint at the airborne armadas to follow.

In those days, crossing the ocean by ship was as natural and inevitable as boarding today's shuttle to fly, let us say, from New York to Boston or Washington. In fact, the word shuttle describes to perfection those flotillas of ocean liners, giant shuttles racketing back and forth on the transatlantic loom, thundering east- and westbound across the world's most dangerous ocean. Regulars called it the Atlantic Ferry, an efficient year-round system of transport that delivered passengers swiftly from Old World to New and back again.

Transatlantic passage was no cruise, no idle dalliance between exotic ports. Rather, it represented a vital maritime enterprise designed to fulfill an apparently insatiable demand. *Everyone* crossed on the liners—businessmen in pursuit of commercial opportunity on the far shore, American tourists anxious to explore Europe or, westbound, immigrants in hopes of finding a better life in these United States. The demand for transatlantic berthing space used to be phenomenal, especially just after the turn of the century when larger and larger vessels had to be launched to accommodate Europe's dispossessed. Millions flocked aboard. The first million-passenger year was

1905, recorded by the United States Immigration Service at Ellis Island.

Since that disparate passenger-load—businessmen, tourists and emigrants—had to be accommodated within a single hull, every vessel was sub-divided into separate classes. These shipboard fiefdoms were entirely self-sufficient, providing each class with its own cabins, open decks, dining saloon, purser's desk, lounge, library and smoking room. The decorative and spatial perquisites of each class were pegged precisely to reflect each class's ticket cost, lavish at the summit but increasingly bleaker and more crowded nearer the bottom. Passengers booked in first class were housed comfortably throughout the superstructure amidships, their deckhouses ringed with convenient promenade decks. Second class was accommodated just aft or below, with a paler carbon copy of public rooms and deckscapes at their disposal. Steerage passengers—the least demanding and, incidentally, most profitable of the ocean liner's clients—occupied Spartan, 'tween-deck leftovers throughout the hull. They took fresh air in well decks fore and aft, plebeian space shared with cargo hatches, booms and winches.

But cruising, even a hundred years ago, has always been one class. Today, only the size and pretension of your cabin varies according to whatever price you have chosen to pay. Outside your cabin threshold, whether it be a modest inside or the owner's suite, you and every one of your fellow passengers are perceived as equals, privileged to roam throughout the vessel's passenger country, indoors and out. Cruising is a democratic far cry from the days of three-class vessels, when lower deck passengers were never permitted to intrude within the domain assigned to shipmates of a superior class.

It always distresses me when people refer to passenger vessels as "floating hotels." Nothing could be further from the truth. What most distinguished ocean liner from hotel was that, uniquely, throughout its capacious black hull, could be found accommodations to suit every purse. Certainly, no hotel offers the same choices; if you do not believe me, try booking a thrifty inside double at the Ritz. Moreover, every meal served in the ocean liner was included in the price of your ticket and every ocean liner occupant checked in and checked out on the same day. On the subject of checking out, if you felt like departing your floating hotel in mid-stay, it could prove problematical. And finally, those aboard an ocean liner were there not as a matter of whim or convenience, they were aboard of necessity, bound irrevocably for another continent.

One inevitable result of that extended mutual journey is that shipboard clients related to one another in a way that fellow occupants of the shorebound hotel almost never do. Hotels neither encourage nor condone social interaction between their clients; aboard ship, the very opposite holds true. Whereas hotel visitors remain essentially anonymous "ships that pass in the night," fellow passengers from day one co-mingle enthusiastically and frequently become lifelong friends.

And it was significant that however accommodated, whether in the splendor of first class or the grime of steerage, every passenger aboard an ocean liner reached port at the same moment, having enjoyed—or endured—an identical span of sea time en route. Although accommodated with comparative degrees of *luxe*, the entire shipload suffered the same wave's impact at the same time, shared (within their respective classes) the same food and chafed at the same discomfort or boredom of sometimes intolerably stormy sea days.

I stress this commonality of experience with reason for it conveys, better than any other way I know, the sense of shipboard's inescapable bonds. All of a hull's occupants—passengers and crew alike—are, in the truest sense of the word, shipmates. The vessel's unyielding steel parameters define as well as promote an irreplaceable interdependence among all who embark.

Consider, for a moment, the classic ocean liner or cruise ship illustration—a distant, sun-struck blur of gleaming white hull and upperworks trailing a wisp of smoke along the horizon. That remote image represents far more than a clichéd vision familiar from playing card or chocolate box; it also evokes a complex, traveling microcosm. If, by some magical legerdemain, you could soar instantaneously across miles of ocean and alight on board, you would immediately become part of a teeming community, voluntarily and cheerfully confined within a benevolent steel prison.

Moreover, you would be miraculously detached from all other life. This is a shipboard characteristic that, curiously, cruise lines seldom mention. Life aboard a passenger ship plodding serenely from horizon to horizon is utterly self-centered. What happens throughout the vessel preoccupies everyone on board to the exclusion of everything else. Embarked passengers, whether on yesterday's ocean liner or today's cruise ship, are devastatingly parochial, consumed with their own affairs. Save for the possibility of variable weather, what exists beyond the ship's railings means little. Regardless that, today, every cabin television set pulls in CNN, regardless that a miniature, faxed *New York Times* appears beneath the cabin door, regardless that friends or family are within easy telephonic reach, events transpiring beyond the horizon seem, at best, inconsequential. Indeed, so pervasive is shipboard's remove from reality that, moments after sailing, pas-

Total cruising contentment: Passengers relax around the pool aboard NORWEGIAN SEA. You could be there.
Barry M Winiker

sengers forget what day it is; hence those seemingly idiotic—to Nonpax—replacement carpets that appear daily within many shipboard elevators announcing not only that it is Wednesday but also "Have a Nice Day."

However enchanting that shipboard ethos, it remains incomprehensible to those who have never experienced it. I have sailed several times with a charming German widow called Hertha Schmitz. *Neu-Pax* Hertha adores cruising but told me one teatime that she no longer shares stories or photographs of her travels with her confirmed *Un-Pax* chums back bei Bonn. As Hertha put it sadly, "They just don't understand."

Another factor guarantees the cruise ship's seaborne limbo. Memories of events that occur aboard a passenger vessel are confined to that voyage and that voyage only. Herewith, an inevitable shipboard scenario: Inquire of any crew member, whether master or maître d'hôtel, about something that took place only one or two cruises earlier and they go blank, unable to recall. Within their day-to-day maritime pressure cooker, anticipation overrides remembrance. Details of previous cruises vanish as irrevocably as that temporary furrow of the vessel's wake. Only today or, better yet, tomorrow count; yesterday is no more.

And once you have disembarked, you too are forgotten. However cordial the master, purser, maître d'hôtel or any of half a dozen dining room captains or stewards, once you have gone ashore, you cease to reckon in that vessel's life. The late great Federico Fellini made an amusing but essentially flawed film about shipboard, the title of which made far more sense than the footage that unspooled after it: *And the Ship Sails On*. So it does, implacably and relentlessly, without you.

An identical myopia about the past infects the corporate mindset ashore. Past cruises are dead, their skeletal remains committed to a statistical catacomb. Anxious to fill berths, cruise lines agonize instead about voyages to come, determined to maximize future revenues. The past, in contemporary parlance, is history, history that remains lamentably undocumented. This neglect is not merely a contemporary cruise line phenomenon, it is as old as the sea itself, where forward has always predominated over aft. Perhaps that is why so much shipboard history remains fragmented and incomplete, because the industry remains irrevocably fixated on the future. All that remains following completion of a cruise is a heap of unclaimed candids jettisoned by the shipboard photographer, as ephemeral as that worldwide avalanche of passenger postcards dispatched by the thousands to friends ashore.

Liners looked and acted differently from cruise ships. They sported sculpted, black hulls capped by hunkered-down superstructure wary of storm. Almost all modern cruise ships tend to virginal white, slab-sided, incredibly tall yet shallow-drafted, with a wedge-shaped bow and bridge screen, the whole production dedicated to sun and frolic. Whereas ocean liners raced, cruise ships dawdle, urgency supplanted by indolence. Though the liner's passengers fumed at delay, their cruising descendants are patently content to drift. Rather than adhering to a relentless, transoceanic schedule, cruising remains a leisurely passenger elective, shipboard for the fun of it.

Yet despite those differences, we still embark within precisely the same maritime ethos as our predecessors did aboard the Atlantic Ferry. Detached from land, we pack most of our shore-based preoccupations: Readers still read, joggers still jog, needle-pointers still needlepoint, sun worshipers still fry themselves and gamblers still wager ceaselessly. Passengers arrange to distract themselves with a plethora of time-fillers—books, crossword puzzles, board games, jigsaw puzzles, bridge, flirting and, always, gossip. And for those lacking their own resources, cruise staffs devise countless additional diversions—quizzes, contests, games and assorted amusements from folding napkins to cooking demonstrations.

Truth to tell, much of the day on board revolves around waiting. Waiting for what? For the next meal, for the next port, for the evening show, for friends to share tea or a drink, for the weather to clear, for the fog to lift, for the sea to subside. And, just as yesterday's passengers filled those waiting hours with knitting, sewing or Raymond Chandler, so today's cruise ship clients are dedicated to knitting, sewing or John Grisham. We embrace our shipboard confinement contentedly, aboard by choice, whereas our parents and grandparents sailed because their voyage was inescapable. But once again, regardless of our contrasting *reasons* for embarkation, we relish identical shipboard rituals, circuiting the decks, lazing in a deck chair, observing our fellow passengers and eating ourselves silly.

Periodically, I run into people who, either ignorant or merely negative, denigrate cruising. Listed alphabetically, their objections might encompass one or more of the following alphabetized descriptives: Adipose, Bored, Claustrophobic, Dumbed, Edgy, Fuming, Grated, Hot, Irritated, Jaded, Knackered, Listless, Malevolent, Nervous, Outraged, Peaked, Querulous, Regimented, Seasick, Tired, Unhappy, Victimized, Woeful, Xhausted, Yowling and Zapped.

By way of response, herewith my alternative alphabet of more accurate cruise modifiers: Adventurous, Blissful, Cossetted, Dreamy, Exhilarated, Fascinated, Gregarious, Happy, Indolent, Joking, Knowledgeable, Learned, Merry, Nonchalant, Optimistic, Pleasured, Quickened, Refreshed, Sunny, Tanned, Unhassled, Vibrant, Welcomed, Xstatic, Youthful and Zealous.

Aboard every passenger vessel, a continuum of endearing passenger dynamics bridges yesterday with today. Nonpax, that same coveted shipboard world awaits your pleasure.

CHAPTER II

Go For It

Make voyages!—Attempt them!—there's nothing else . . .

—Tennessee Williams, *Camino Real*

A traveler has a right to relate and embellish his adventures as he pleases, and it is very impolite to refuse that deference and applause they deserve.

—Rudolf Erich Raspe, *Travels of Baron Munchausen*

I always keep firmly in mind what must be described as The Case of the Cape Cod Kibitzers.

It happened one night back in October of 1987. ROYAL VIKING SEA was returning to New York through the Cape Cod Canal, concluding a fall foliage cruise to Canada and back. En route north, we had transited the canal by daylight but on the southbound leg, we passed through after dark.

Though I had crossed over the canal by car hundreds of times, I had never before actually sailed through that ambitious, man-made ditch separating Cape Cod from mainland Massachusetts. On this particular evening, our weather could not have been more ideal: The autumn air was cool but not bitter and we chased a full harvest moon hovering just above pine-forested profiles along our nocturnal route.

As we glided through the dark, passengers lined the promenade decks just as spectators apparently lined both shores. Though unseen, they were not unheard. What mystified everyone on board was the torrent of insults and epithets hurled across waters separating ship from shore. Neither space nor propriety permits verbatim reproduction but suffice to say, those invisible watchers neglected not one entry from the taboo roster of four-letter words, in vociferous, inventive and articulate combination.

That abusive barrage continued the length of our transit. It was not until we were approaching the canal's southernmost bridge at Bourne that one anonymous, agonized voice rang out from shore, momentarily in the clear.

"It must be nice to have money!" was that adolescent *cri de coeur*.

Mystery solved. For those presumably beer-fuelled townies lining the banks of their canal, the glittering vision sliding past conjured up all the romantic allure of the unobtainable. Clearly, we aboard ROYAL VIKING SEA were perceived as the haves, while our opposite numbers ashore saw themselves as the perpetual have-nots.

I wish it were somehow possible to track down that candid young man from Bourne, whoever and wherever he is. By now, he may well be married and raising a family. But he and all his canal-side buddies should realize, as do millions of their fellow countrymen, that embarkation aboard a cruise ship today is not restricted to the rich nor does it necessarily imply upper-crust exclusivity.

The days when cruise passengers were perennially characterized as "newly-weds or nearly-deads" are long gone. Cruising has metamorphosed into a splendidly economical travel opportunity for a broad sociological spectrum of Americans. Today's passenger lists transcend what might once have seemed a privileged minority, made up instead of an infinite cross-section of people from all walks of life, from truck driver to tycoon, from salesman to society matron, from retro freaks to retirees. As we surmount the millennium, the pleasures of shipboard are extraordinarily and universally available.

And what an incredible and unique travel bargain a ship represents! Back in 1985, I convinced a dear school friend of mine in England to board a passenger ship for the first time. Nonpax John and Roma Cresswell were comfortably off, had been everywhere and done everything, everything, that is, *except book a cabin*. After some gentle but repetitively persistent persuasion, they decided at the last minute that they would sail with Mary and myself aboard QUEEN ELIZABETH 2 from Southampton to New York. As it happened, Newpax Cresswells inadvertently got more than they bargained for. One unbidden transatlantic surprise for that entire shipload was Hurricane Gloria; but that is another story, told in a later chapter.

What concerns me at the moment was our first night's dinner up in QE2's Queens Grill. Mary, Roma and I began with caviar, an indulgence that John, with a jaundiced eye, refused. At the end of the meal, John reminded me pointedly that "when the check comes, remember that I did *not* have any caviar."

I could scarcely believe my ears: Well-traveled, sophisticated and debonair John Cresswell was fretting about the bill for his first shipboard dinner.

"My dear fellow," I hastened to reassure him, "you paid for this dinner and, indeed, every course of every meal to come when you bought your ticket in London."

Nonpax all, take heed: Every scrap of food aboard a cruise ship,

Enormous amounts of food are endemic to cruising. And it is all included in the price of your ticket. *Author's Collection*

whether consumed in the dining room, out on deck or delivered to your cabin, is included with the price of your fare. (The only single exception to this rule might be an ice cream cone ordered around the swimming pool.) To my mind, that unique, gastronomic largess remains one of the outstanding pluses among cruising's multitudinous pluses. Listen to some of the others.

You embark aboard your floating paradise. You unpack (only once). As just elaborated, everything you eat on board—and, trust me, it will be a great deal—has already been paid for; so too has a lavish profusion of music and nightly entertainment; so too has your effortless progression from port to port.

Quite recently, on board GRAND PRINCESS at the conclusion of a westbound repositioning crossing, my wife Mary was astonished to hear passengers complaining at the cashier's desk that they had thought their shipboard laundry and dry cleaning had been gratis. To avoid misunderstandings of that kind, it is as well to understand those items for which you will be expected to pay. *Not included* as part of your cruise fare will be the following:

* All drinks, soft or hard, whether served in a bar, out on deck, in the dining room or delivered to your cabin. The only exception to this rule would be drinks on board upscale, high per-diem vessels where they are often provided free.
* Pictures taken by a roving team of talented shipboard photographers. However many they snap, you are not obliged to buy any unless you wish to. (Doris Bickwit, an experienced shipmate with whom we used regularly to sail on Royal Viking tonnage, systematically bought and destroyed every unflattering photograph she could find of herself displayed on the photographer's rack.)
* All laundry or dry cleaning. Washing machines and dryers are available on board with which you can do your own laundry if you prefer. In fact, shipboard laundromats fulfil the function of communal village wells, the source of much passenger-exchanged news and gossip.
* All charges at the medical center, whether for doctor's appointment, prescription or supplies.
* All beauty salon services, from haircut or permanent to massage or elaborate spa treatment.

* All shore excursions and/or shuttle busses organized by the cruise line.
* All items purchased in the shops on board.
* Whatever monies you choose to risk in the casino, whether slot machines or gaming tables or, in the lounge, while playing bingo or horse-racing.
* Canapés if you decide to give a cocktail party.
* All tips at voyage's end, with which you will reward your cabin steward and dining room waiters. Tips are an ancient shipboard tradition to be exhaustively discussed in Chapter IX.

But every other delight of your floating vacation has been paid for. Incidentally, in all the books I have written about shipboard, I try never to mention prices. They change so drastically over the decades that what might have seemed an extravagance in the 1930s would seem ludicrously inexpensive in terms of today's dollars. For example, during the depths of the depression, you could book the least expensive cabin aboard dear old MAURETANIA for a 9-day cruise—from New York to Nassau and back—for $108. Would that same dollar amount offset your drinking and/or gambling budget for one day on a contemporary cruise ship? Perhaps.

Incidentally, you will live aboard ship in a sensibly cashless environment. All cruise ship prices, regardless of nationality, are computed in dollars and all your expenses—whether in the shops, shore excursions or bars—will be electronically charged at the time of purchase to your shipboard account. Upon embarkation, an imprint of your credit card will be taken so that the cruise's final aggregate charges can be automatically charged to your card. To forestall any possible misunderstandings, a copy of your bill will appear under your cabin door in the early hours of the day you finally disembark.

I have found that money, and how each of us chooses to dispense it, remains one of the most subjective, not to say secretive, vagaries of human behavior. There are hundreds of thousands of astute marketers out there who try their level best to guess how much money we feel comfortable spending on everything from a certain model of car to a specific brand of toothpaste, from an airline preference to favorite running shoes. Which brands we ultimately choose and why we prefer them remain extremely personal or even quixotic choices, arising out of the sometimes manipulated but essentially instinctive preferences of every individual or, more likely, individual couples. And the secret of locking in a consumer's brand loyalty remains of keenest interest to producers of every service and product in the world.

Interminable financial debate consumes the lives of all paired consumers. Research suggests that married couples agonize more about money than any other issue affecting their joint lives, more than children, dwelling or even the family car. How much should they should spend on what, whether to splurge or economize and deciding what specific expense seems an extravagance or a mutually acceptable indulgence.

The same debate governs the choice and price of a vacation. What do couples consider expensive and what a bargain? In that regard, compared with a stay at any resort, hotel, dude ranch or chartered yacht, cruising remains *the* unequivocal bargain. Moreover, apart from the dollars expended, shipboard's unique state of grace, as I have attempted to explain, includes so many potent intangibles.

Put it this way. Every one of the ports or countries listed along every cruise ship itinerary can, in all honesty, be reached more swiftly and cheaply by air. Nevertheless, nothing is more alluring than embarking aboard a ship for traditional arrival at those same destinations. The romance—if any—of touching down at an airport pales into insignificance beside the evocative thrill of approaching and entering a port by sea; indeed, the very rhythm of a cruise, with its alternating sea days and port days, is one of shipboard's most seductive aspects. No other means of travel offers a comparable mystique, no experience imparts the same extraordinary degree of community and delight. Once ensconced aboard a cruise ship, you will derive not only more enjoyment, you will also derive incomparable dividends in terms of cruising's three irreplaceable Rs: Recreation, Relaxation and Renewal. Having taken the plunge and invested in a cruise ticket, you will embark in a fever of anticipation. By the same token, I guarantee you will disembark not only exhilarated but also a confirmed cruise addict. Be warned: shipboard is a compelling—if benign—narcotic, one that will oblige you to seek cumulative cruising fixes forever.

One caveat of which Nonpax should be aware: Like any new boy or girl at a school, you may suffer a momentary loss of face in that you will boast no prior shipboard experience to share with your fellow passengers. Alan and Nancy Anderson, dear friends of mine, once sailed with us aboard SEABOURN PRIDE from Fort Lauderdale to Lisbon. It was only their second cruise and they reported after one day's chatting around the vessel that they felt ill-at-ease in that they were not as experienced as their fellow passengers aboard, particularly our Oldpax stronghold.

I should have warned them. Newpax and Oldpax alike love nothing more than cruise-dropping—musing, raving or complaining about prior ships, prior ports and prior cruises. They invariably rehash their cruise credentials the moment they meet anyone aboard their latest ship. I suggested to the Andersons (a) that you tolerate these presumptive cruise bores and (b) rest assured that within a short time—immediately following this cruise, in fact—you will join their ranks, disseminating to all who will listen your accumulated wisdom and expertise about life aboard your last ship.

A final word to coax you across that gangway, particularly if you are envisioning a summer cruise. If you can manage it, take every member of your family. Ships are a paradise for children; they can—and do—run free and will find the whole cruise experience captivating. Moreover, your life as a parent will be made easy. Every cruise line employs numbers of cruise staff whose job it is to provide amusement and entertainment for both young and even younger passengers. Small fry report happily each day to a supervised playroom staffed by experienced counselors while teenagers enjoy their own shipboard hangout, complete with rock music, MTV, movies and programs of their own where things are kept purposely laid back and, always, cool. Your children will inevitably reproach you for going on a cruise without them but will remain eternally grateful if you bring them along.

Another avenue of booking a cabin that you may choose to explore is joining an existing group. There are countless offerings—museums, clubs or alumni groups who have block-booked accommodations at reduced prices if you sail with them. But if you would prefer to choose your own ships rather than the one that group has already ordained, then recruit some like-minded friends and form your own group.

In sum, dismiss all anxiety. Telephone your travel agent this minute and go for it!

CHAPTER III

But Which Ship and Where To?

The sea is at its best at London, near midnight, when you are within the arms of a capacious chair, before a glowing fire, selecting phases of the voyage you will never make.

—H. M. Tomlinson, *The Sea and the Jungle*, 1912

The cruising world is your oyster. You can embark aboard any one of dozens of cruise ships for either three months or three days, depending on the amount of time and money at your disposal. The longer of the two alternatives would tie you up for a leisurely quarter-year at sea while, over three days, you would merely sample a couple of Caribbean islands or, on the west coast, a Mexican port or two.

In all honesty, I would recommend neither. The thousands of dollars required for even the most modest berth aboard a cruise ship circling the globe represent a sizable investment which, as your maiden venture, might plunge you into deeper and more challenging waters than you wish. My advice? Save that long circumnavigation for later, after you have gotten some shorter cruises under your belt. I once met a first-time passenger aboard ROTTERDAM, embarked for a world cruise. She was there because she had won a $26,000 jackpot on a nickel slot machine out in

Las Vegas and decided to blow most of it on a world cruise. It was quite clear to me she found herself out of her depth; as indolent weeks rolled by, she remained an awkward outsider on the fringes of what is really an exclusive club.

And at the other end of the chronological spectrum, three- and/or four-day cruises may also prove keen disappointments for beginners. Although cruise lines selling short cruises may well find fault with my logic, let me suggest that less than a week's cabin tenancy is inadequate for a novice Nonpax. Admittedly, your abbreviated stay on board could conceivably whet your shipboard appetite but my guess is that you will more likely disembark if not unhappy at least unfulfilled.

Let me explain. The downer of the three-day itinerary is its brevity, in both days and sea miles. Since the vessel must achieve a suitable port within overnight reach of Florida, Nassau remains your inevitable destination of choice. Your ship sails from Miami in late afternoon, spending its first night creeping at an irritating snail's pace towards the nearby Bahamas.

Purists might carp: What difference does it make at what speed your vessel moves? Trust me, a great deal. A ship dawdling at only a few knots seems somehow incapacitated whereas a ship bound briskly for the horizon exhilarates. Small but elemental maritime nuances of this kind, you will discover, do matter.

You will awake the following morning tied up alongside in Nassau, the Bahamian capital. You and your ship will remain there for the entire day, permitting you either to explore the island or remain on board, enjoying the amenities of the ship. You and your fellow passengers will have ample time to investigate Nassau fully but rest assured, apart from some gewgaws from the pier-side straw market, you will return with little to show for your efforts.

By nightfall, with all passengers back on board and ready for sea, the vessel proceeds to its next destination. You are bound overnight for Freeport, another snail-like progression towards another day tied up alongside. You will sail again at dusk for a third day, either anchored off an out island or, if you are lucky, a full day at sea.

Out islands have become standard Caribbean cruise line offerings, the first one inaugurated by the Norwegian Cruise Line in 1980. Customarily but not always in the Bahamas, out islands are low-lying, sandy atolls, discreetly developed as "desert" islands, designed for the exclusive use of ships of their owning company. A barbecue lunch is offered ashore, before and after which you can swim, snorkel, sunbathe or snooze.

The following dawn, you will find yourself back in Miami and off the ship. The bulk of your cruise, whether three- or four-day, has been spent tied up. You have sailed almost exclusively in the dark, your voyage so brief that you will have derived only a fleeting sense of shipboard's magic.

In their defense, companies do try to compress what they describe as "the full cruise experience" into those truncated sojourns but, however much bingo and buffet they pack in, it seems a losing battle. Although short cruises make sense as getaways for experienced passengers, I strongly recommend that Nonpax raise their sights for their first shipboard immersion. At stake is the potential for an indifferent first impression; for beginners to savor half a week aboard their first ship pursuing an essentially pedestrian itinerary may sour them forever.

In truth, disappointing Nassau serves America's cruise ship market as an inferior substitute for embargoed Havana. When and if relations between Cuba and the United States are ever normalized, ship-rich Nassau will become an instant ghost port as every three- and four-day cruise will flock to Havana instead. Rest assured that charts, schedules, excursions and port arrangements for Cuba are poised and waiting in all Floridian cruise lines' contingency files.

Incidentally, for the record, at the end of every cruise regardless of length, vessels "turnaround", as they say, on the same day. The old passenger-load disembarks in the morning and a new one embarks that same afternoon. Although some long-range ships still occasionally spend an overnight in port—Venice, Hong Kong and New York offer rare exceptions—it makes better economic sense for the companies to keep their ships, like aircraft, in almost constant motion. In the old days along New York's piers, coal-burning Atlantic liners used to tie up for several days while laundry, provisions, mail and hundreds of tons of coal were laboriously winched on board. But today, with many provisions frozen, laundry washed on board, mail destined for airports and diesel oil the fuel of choice, the invariable cruise ship rule is in at dawn, out by dusk.

I suggest that for your maiden cruise you book at the least a seven-day Caribbean cruise; the weather is predictably good year-round—save for early fall's hurricane possibilities—and those turquoise waters remain universally benign. During your week on board, your vessel will make several island calls.

An elemental division characterizes all passenger ship itineraries around the globe. Such are cruising's inescapable logistics that days aboard your ship will be of two kinds, either sea days or port days. Just as one is quite different from the other, so one would not be possible without the other. Nonpax should fully understand and appreciate these differences before selecting any cruise.

Let me confess immediately to a strong emotional bias in favor of sea days. For my money, sea days are to be treasured while too many port days must be endured. I am frank to admit that this is an intensely personal reaction and in articulating it, I have no intention of selling short the many intriguing possibilities that await beyond gangway's end.

In a subsequent chapter, we shall deal exhaustively with the subject of shorex (cruisespeak for shore excursions). And although the opening lines of my introduction suggested that cruising is passenger, cruising is also very much port and always has been. The idea of taking cruises originated in the mid-nineteenth century as a novelty, a largely educational adventure wherein liners were detached from transoceanic routes and deployed to carry curious passengers to a variety of cultural or historic destinations achievable by sea. In a world devoid of the instant communication with which we are surfeited today, our forebears boarded cruise ships *to go and see for themselves*. They visited the Holy Land, they explored the ruins of classical antiquity crowding Mediterranean shores, they steamed through exotic waters of every kind, from far Pacific to remote Scandinavia. Going ashore then was an adventure and, for many of my fellow passengers, it remains one to the present. I too have enjoyed my share of rewarding excursions ashore but for the most part feel that port days too often serve to disrupt the pleasanter sequence of sea days.

Let me put my case. First, understand that ships are sea creatures which flourish best in their element. A passenger vessel under way is working exactly as its naval architects and designers intended. For Newpax and Oldpax alike, the time-honored and satisfying rituals of shipboard enrich every aspect of their floating milieu. On a ship under way at sea, you stroll around the deck, take the sun, enjoy a leisurely meal. The shops are open for busi-

Simpatico days at sea: The on-deck scene is languid and serene, whether surveying the sea or, sun-baked, engrossed in a thriller.
Lothar Simon and Author's Collection

ness, pools are filled with or surrounded by sun worshipers, walkers and joggers circuit the promenades past deck chair occupants devouring books. Indoors, lectures, demonstrations and meetings hold sway and there is always a favored slot machine to be primed in the casino. In the theater, hard-working dancers and singers rehearse yet another evening's treat to come. Along cabin corridors, steward or stewardess puts cabins to rights save where a doorknob's *Do Not Disturb* betrays late-sleepers.

Self-contained within and without, our ship bowls along imperturbably. Over each railing, we can watch sundered waters slip by, hissing where foam-flecked waves recoil from the implacable rampart of our moving hull. Overhead, funnel smoke shimmers and dissipates before the scouring ocean breeze and a dome of purest cerulean blue mates with surrounding horizon. Our perception of that fixed sea/sky margin is rhythmically at odds with the gentle, hypnotic lift and fall of the bow, motion as old as the waves. All is at peace. The vessel, her crew and her passengers are all functioning precisely as Triton and Poseidon intended they should. One sea day is glorious, two sublime, three, four, five or six, perfection.

But, inevitably, a port intrudes. Perhaps the cruelest intrusion is not the port itself but the inescapably unsettling *prospect* of a port. I have observed the same phenomenon time after time. However blithely our ship is proceeding across a flawless expanse of deep water, on the afternoon before a port call, that precious shipboard fabric begins unraveling. A persistent, nagging anxiety suffuses the vessel.

No one is immune. Officers, whether on the bridge or in the engine room, become preoccupied with harbor entrance, bunkering (refueling) or taking on fresh water. Senior hotel staff worry about disembarking or newly-embarking passengers as well as customs and immigration formalities; their juniors unlimber foreign stamps and currency. While master and safety officer formulate plans for a crew boat drill in port, staff captain and bosun schedule bouts of shipboard maintenance. Chef and galley staff fret about re-provisioning. The crew checklist of port-induced disruptions is unending.

Unease pervades the passenger body as well. Port anticipation precipitates a ship-wide dither. Which shore excursion are we booked on? When does it leave? When will it return? Should we just explore the port on our own? How early do we have to get up for breakfast? How will we change money? What will the weather be like? What should we wear? Will sandals adequate for a stroll from cabin to pool stand up to the rigors of clambering around ruins ashore? On port day eve, plaintive queries are unceasing.

Passengers booked on tours may be off the ship for half the day or as much as eight hours; their reluctance to relinquish already comforting shipboard links is palpable. I sense what nags at them is a worrying exchange of status. On board, they know the ropes and, even more important, are known; ashore they will become strangers in the midst of unknown turmoil.

By dinner time, the vessel has transmogrified from haven to hive, indolence supplanted by angst. The level and intensity of conversation in the dining room that night is tauter and more querulous. After-dinner entertainment falls short, with early bed a restlessly preferred option.

The following day, everyone is milling about at dawn. Gone the languid peace of the sea day. A remote, alien humidity indicates that shell plating has been breached for disembarkation. Loudspeakers summon delinquent tour members with a persistent drone. Once the tour busses have departed, the vessel subsides into torpor. A few holdouts remain on board.

What could be better, the neophyte might fantasize: Here I am on a luxurious vessel, tied up alongside in a tropical port, free to go ashore for sightseeing, beach time or shopping. What's the difference—alongside or at sea, the ship is the same ship, is it not?

Not really. Tied up, a cruise ship is moribund. Shops and casino are closed, crew and passengers are dispersed and the contagious rhythm of shipboard dynamics quelled. Everything is closed down and inoperative. Only at day's end, when all have re-embarked and we have regained the open sea, will the vessel return to the life it and its clients deserve.

I hope Nonpax readers will grasp these essential contrasts between sea and port days. Regardless that you keep those distinctions firmly in mind, let me make an iron-clad prediction. Once you have pored over rival company brochures and selected your first cruise, odds are that you will zero in on a vessel that calls at the largest number of ports during its week-long voyage. Marketing strategists at every Caribbean cruise line know full well that Nonpax—and even those Newpax who have not yet seen the light—set great store in maximizing their most advantageous geographical return. Since novice passengers are seduced by port numbers, the marketing dogma goes, we shall cram as many as possible within our cruise's week.

Typically, vessels sailing from Puerto Rico's San Juan enjoy the densest selection of adjacent ports, all within an effortless overnight sail. As a result, many San Juan-based, seven-day itineraries start with one day at sea before spending the balance of the week calling at five consecutive ports. In musical terms, your cruise opera begins with a bravura sea day overture, before deteriorating into five turgid acts of a port a day.

To innocent Nonpax, this may sound irresistible. Five ports must be superior to four, four ports an improvement over three.

At work here is the scalp factor: Novice Nonpax want to fly home at cruise's end with a collection of ports hanging like scalps from their belts, the more the better.

But consider the downside. For nearly your entire week on board, you will be immobilized in port, just as though you were on a three- or four-day cruise, baking at a pier, inert and closed down. The vessel will only come to life at dusk as it shuttles to the next port. Moreover, scalp-gatherers will discover that their full belt comes at a price. Up early, they abandon ship for a wilting day ashore before debilitated return. Port marathons are cumulatively exhausting. Saddest of all, the whole *raison d'être* of being aboard ship is suffering from an overdose of ashore. That irreplaceable sense of traveling community, an intrinsic and historic aspect of shipboard, never really coalesces.

Herewith another iron-clad prediction: After your first cruise, as budding Newpax, my guess is that in brochures to come, you will tot up sea days rather than port days. Keep in mind that cruise lines go to incredible lengths to make their ships as commodious, comfortable and amusing as possible; it seems a fearful waste to neglect those delights for the dubious return of daily fixes ashore.

This chapter posed the question—what ship and where to? It does not really matter. Ships are ships and you will derive equal pleasure from any number of them. Moreover, where they go, you will come to appreciate, matters less than how they go. What matters terribly and what every Nonpax should fully comprehend, is the crucial difference between days under glorious way and days mired in port.

CHAPTER IV

WHAT TO PACK—AND WHY

First, let's settle the eternal question of what to wear. Well! That, as you know, is a difficult thing for one woman to tell another! A Hollywood star may not find it hard to tell you "How to be glamorous" but my problem is to suit all tastes, all ages, all purses in all sorts of weather. Let me emphasize that you can really have a better time if you are comfortably dressed.

—Esther Boyer, Social Directress, FRANCONIA World Cruise, 1934

I defy anyone in the world to derive any amusement from coping with luggage day after day at docks and railway stations and frontiers, from unpacking and re-packing a mysteriously increasing collection of books and drawing materials and photographs and dirty clothes and antiques.

—Evelyn Waugh, *In Defense of Pleasure Cruising*, 1930

The first thing of all,
When booking a cruise,
Is race to the mall
For lots of new shoes.

—John Maxtone-Graham, circa 1985

Beware of enterprises that require new clothes.

—Henry David Thoreau

While waiting for an aircraft to take off, nothing distresses me more than observing the number of passengers thronging aboard, apparently burdened with everything they own. Despite repeated company admonishments about only two items of hand luggage, passengers routinely struggle down aircraft aisles dragging wheeled suitcases, their shoulders festooned with garment bags, duffel bags, briefcases and computers.

Why are they reluctant to consign anything to the baggage hold? Have they been burned by airlines that lost or delayed their luggage, can they not bear to be separated from their belongings or do they have such a hectic schedule that a carousel wait is anathema? I am never sure. Most unsettling to me—fortunately never put to the test—is that in the event of an emergency, I suspect those with the largest overhead stash will be the most reluctant to evacuate briskly and without question.

Clearly, those luggage indulgers have embarked on the wrong conveyance. Aboard cruise ships, no limitation exists; moreover, it will be manhandled on board and delivered to your cabin by other hands than yours. When cruising, the sky—in addition to your cabin size and clothing inventory—is the limit.

We cannot properly tackle the subject of passenger luggage without delving, yet again, into ocean liner history. Aboard the earliest steamships, everyone embarked with what was called a steamer trunk, essentially a footlocker never more than 14 inches high, so designed that it fitted beneath the 15-inch-high horsehair cabin sofa paralleling the cabin's double-decker bunks. This was the nineteenth century's logistical equivalent of the twentieth century's overnight suitcase obliged to fit beneath an aircraft seat. But unlike aircraft, there was no leniency aboard ship. If the trunk would *not* slide beneath the sofa, there was no overhead

Typical of thousands of luggage tags used aboard every ocean liner, this one specified that the trunk should remain in the hold until deposited on New York's pier. *Author's Collection*

alternative and parking it elsewhere in a cramped cabin was problematical.

Packed within the steamer trunk were clothes selected for durability but seldom style. Early steamers reeked pervasively of steam, oil, coal, tar, drains, cabbage, vomit and, perforce, an overridingly stern antiseptic. That inescapable steamship miasma so infused the fabric of passenger clothing that the contents of a steamer trunk were restricted to sea use only. Having crossed eastbound, disembarking Americans would pack their noisome steamer clothing back into steamer trunks for storage in company warehouses, to be retrieved when re-embarking for passage back to New York.

If passengers traveled with more than one trunk, they were tagged with one of two company-issued labels, either WANTED ON THE VOYAGE or NOT WANTED ON THE VOYAGE. Those WANTED would be delivered to the cabin while those NOT WANTED were consigned to the hold. Passengers would not be reunited with hold baggage until they found it deposited—with luck—beneath the appropriate initial strung overhead along the pier when they disembarked.

Those hanging alphabets were commonplace in every North Atlantic terminus. Passenger Jones would find his luggage beneath the letter "J" while Passenger Smith searched beneath "S." Some tried beating the system. Rather than muck in with other J's or S's, passengers requested "X" stickers from their bedroom steward, ensuring that longshoremen would deposit their luggage in solitary prominence beneath that seldom-employed letter. But it proved a diminishing advantage; so many learned the ruse that "X" became equally crowded. Nowadays, cruise ships identify off-loaded luggage with color-coded baggage tags instead of lettered stickers; the overhead alphabets of old are no more.

Shipboard's next baggage generation featured wardrobe trunks, strapped, banded monsters that reigned as undisputed kings of the luggage menagerie. Wardrobe trunks are seldom seen today unless consigned to the sidewalk awaiting garbage pickup or, papered with exotic labels, employed as evocative window dressing for department store displays. (If, among the labels, you ever spot an "X" sticker, the trunk's owner was a knowledgeable traveler.)

Always WANTED ON THE VOYAGE, these luggage behemoths would be shoehorned into the cabin and parked in a corner. (If you visit QUEEN MARY in Long Beach today, note the generous width of her first class corridors, designed so that two wardrobe trunks could pass abreast with ease.) Standing open like a giant dictionary, wardrobe trunks were seldom unpacked. One side was equipped with bureau drawers, the other with a hanging rod. A large, foldout box at the bottom of the hanging space accommodated shoes. Although long evening dresses fared better in a cabin closet, the wardrobe trunk's drawers remained a useful bureau adjunct. On disembarkation day, the giant trunk would be swung shut, locked and tagged, to be delivered either to the pier or into the boat train's freight car for shipment to one's London or Paris hotel.

Concomitant to all the movement of passenger trunks in those halcyon days was an efficient trunk delivery service from home to pier to hotel and back. Railway Express—sadly no longer in existence—provided efficient trucking service linking railway station with pier. Since then, with station supplanted by airport and train eclipsed by aircraft, everything must fit inside a car's trunk or an aircraft's hold. Trunks are nearly extinct today; only children going to camp seem to use them. In truth, trunks would overwhelm the available floor space in most cruising cabins; unpacked suitcases must fit beneath the bed, seldom more than ten inches high at best.

Wardrobe containers of a different kind still play a starring role in the world cruise drama, those annual extravaganzas that start circumnavigating the globe every January. Once each year, evading the bitter cold of New York or Southampton's gray murk, half a dozen upscale cruise ships chase the sun around the world until early spring. World cruise Oldpax ladies, anticipating dozens of dressy evenings, must pack dozens of dressy dresses. We must assume that since they can afford to spend a quarter of a year at sea, they also rejoice in a wardrobe inventory to match.

To accommodate them, there are specialist firms somewhere in Long Island that rent large plywood costume boxes equipped with hanging rods. The box arrives empty to the client's house. Once it has been packed, the firm then retrieves it and delivers it to the appropriate pier. There, longshoremen and stewards make sure it reaches the right cabin. Once emptied—assuming there is sufficient closet space—the empty wardrobe box is consigned to the hold against the day of disembarkation when the entire logistical process must be repeated in reverse.

Every world cruise vessel has its own story of self-indulgent, clothes-rich (or just plain rich) Oldpax ladies who overcome the hanging limitation of their cabin by booking the adjoining one, transforming it into an oversize, supplementary closet to accommodate the balance of their traveling finery.

But for the vast majority of Newpax, world cruises exist only as rare if enviable anomalies. For the purposes of this volume, we shall deal with clothing required for cruises lasting either a week or at most, a fortnight. Given that shrinkage of time and space, we shall lower our sights from wardrobe box to suitcase.

One of the sad things that has happened to contemporary luggage is that, nowadays, leather is almost completely impractical.

Some years ago, Mary and I bought three large, matching suitcases from a New York purveyor of smart luggage. They are sublime creations, made up of cream-colored goat skin, every edge banded in brown calf. Excellent hardware and hinges adorn the exterior while inside, linen lining and generous straps keep clothing pristine. Each brass-mounted carrying handle incorporates a cushioned, buttery-soft leather grip.

Contrasting baggage: *above* The author and his wife pose with "the luggage of the whore" aboard QUEEN ELIZABETH 2, sailing in and out of New York. *below* The compromise, soft black nylon suitcases with a bright yellow MG painted on the side. *Ian Maxtone-Graham and Author's Collection*

I have made three discoveries since that extravagant purchase. First, in every film portraying ridiculously extravagant travelers, those same suitcases always appear; obviously, set decorators find them irresistibly appropriate as upscale props. Second, my French son-in-law Bernard took one look at all that goat skin and pronounced it immediately "the luggage of the whore." Third, for the past few years, those suitcases have rarely left our house.

Why? Quite simply because they are so vulnerable to abuse. Once, at London's Ritz, they were inadvertently stacked in a luggage room beneath a leaking pipe. The topmost one suffered an unsightly, verdigris-colored stain which a distraught assistant concierge tried unsuccessfully to remove. But Ritz notwithstanding, wherever we take them, those glorious suitcases are mercilessly scratched, scarred and scuffed on every surface. Maybe longshoremen or baggage handlers, given temporary custody of "the luggage of the whore," enjoy wreaking gleeful class vengeance on it whenever possible. Whatever the travel wear and tear, it is clear that the luggage was designed more for show than serviceability. I still recall asking the salesman if the brown trim were vinyl or leather. "Leather, of course, sir!" he sniffed disdainfully. Were it serviceable and resilient vinyl, all those banded margins would have survived far more successfully.

However, they offer one curious advantage aboard ship. Whenever we disembark in New York, there is no need to search for either suitcase, longshoreman or trolley. Some enterprising stevedore always lines up all three of them on a trolley, awaiting only the pleasure of the obviously affluent owners before whisking us all through customs to what he obviously expects will be at least a Daimler.

So choose your shipboard luggage with care and eschew vulnerable (however beautiful) leather. Opt instead for something in stout, dark-colored nylon. Black is my, as well as most people's, choice so I have painted the initials "MG" in bright yellow on both sides to alleviate the carousel vigil. The only hard luggage I recommend might be one of those indestructible jobs that in television commercials serve as playthings for caged gorillas. Luggage destined for cruise ships must endure two successive purgatories because almost all of today's cruise passengers fly to and from their vessel.

Once you reach the pier, Nonpax, make sure that your tickets and passports are *not* packed inside the heavy luggage you surrender to the longshoremen. Traditionally, you tip them. In fact, those cheerful rogues will await you, smiling with open palms beneath large signs announcing that their services are complimentary.

On board, investigating your cabin and waiting for your suitcases to reappear, do not feel obligated to tip the ship's luggage team who deliver them to your cabin. Many will parrot a well-oiled litany: "You won't be seeing us again." A few psychologically attuned shipboard baggage handlers have been known to withhold one outstanding suitcase. As sailing time approaches and passenger distress has ratcheted up sufficiently, they suddenly "find" that elusive missing piece and willingly accept the wads of currency its appearance engenders. In sum, give those luggage stewards something if you feel like it but know that you are not obliged to.

A few years ago, I embarked aboard CRYSTAL SYMPHONY at the start of a world cruise from Los Angeles. Ominously, not one suitcase appeared in our cabin. Frantic as departure time approached, I searched the adjacent pier shed in vain. We were, after all, not merely island-hopping around the Caribbean, we were poised on the brink of the vast Pacific; had our suitcases not been embarked, they would not have reached us for days. Not until after we had sailed did I finally discover them, heaped mystifyingly on the bed of a distant, unoccupied cabin.

Aboard almost any Caribbean-bound ship, you sometimes find an understandably disgruntled passenger couple whose luggage has gone astray and not reached the pier in time. Those unfortunate souls spend the first days of their cruise either wearing their plane clothes or disbursing unanticipated funds throughout the shipboard shops, making do with replacements until their errant suitcases catch up with them at the next island. These episodes are thankfully rare, especially since the demise of Eastern Airlines.

Since the ocean liner's trunks have metamorphosed into the cruise ship's suitcases, how many does one need for a week at sea? Quite honestly, it depends on your wardrobe discretion. Our dear friend, the late Anne Lincoln, with whom we used to sail frequently, always baffled us by arriving on board burdened with only one small 1950s vintage, Oshkosh suitcase of the kind luggage salesmen describe as a two-suiter. That was her entire *impedimenta*, as the Romans called baggage. How Anne did it, we never found out. Suffice to say, she always appeared at the lunch or dinner table impeccably and appropriately dressed; moreover, few if any garments were repeated. Admittedly, from a purely masculine perspective, women's dresses consume far less space than suits; so too do their shoes. But I have always wished fervently that before she left us, Anne had shared her single suitcase strategy. Her economy and ingenuity were remarkable, akin to the magical, apparently bottomless portmanteau that Mary Poppins unpacked when she first arrived in the Banks' nursery.

Deprived of both Anne Lincoln and Mary Poppins's sleight of hand, other packing dodges for cruises should be shared. A retired school teacher, traveling on a slender budget, booked a minimum inside cabin for LACONIA's first world cruise of 1922. She brought with her a dome-topped, oak-lathed trunk that contained an odious collection of her old and obviously much-worn clothing, akin to steamer clothing of yore. She wore each item for several days before, by design, hurling it over the side and replacing it with whatever she found down on the next packed layer. Practicing this Spartan economy of dress, she and her shabby dishabille circumnavigated the globe without endearing herself to any fellow passengers.

Rather the same system in reverse was once recommended to me as an ingenious means of packing by Derek Mann, a friend and veteran cruise director. As you use a set of clothes, Derek advised, discard it folded in the bottom of your empty suitcase. By the cruise's last day, you will be fully packed to go home.

For our sins, Mary and I travel heavy rather than light. The only limitation about luggage for even a week's tenancy aboard ship is the size and number of your suitcase(s), the size of your closet and the number of available drawers. As it happens, even modestly priced cabins come equipped with sufficient storage space to accommodate the most self-indulgent passenger.

I cannot think that Nonpax need pointers about packing but I will share a couple of tricks for what they're worth. Shirts—which I iron and fold myself—survive best in a soft suitcase if cushioned, overlapping, between the protective legs of folded trousers. Similarly, I organize neckties into a quarter of their length and wrap the entire bundle tightly within the cocooning bulk of a sweater. Long ago, my tailor advised packing any jacket with its collar raised and one shoulder snugged inside out within its opposite number; then, if the whole garment is folded vertically once again, it can be unpacked and worn immediately without pressing. Shoes, with trees, are heavy but there is no escaping that; soft shoes can be buttressed internally with balled up socks. And herewith, a plug for humble espadrilles, a pair of which pack flat so neatly and economically; although useless for early morning wet decks, these rope-soled, canvas shoes from Spain otherwise make ideal shipboard footgear.

Two final caveats: I would strongly advise doing all your packing from home in one session. Committing clothes and possessions to suitcases over more than one day can lead to fatal omissions. I keep in my travel diary a list of items that Mary and I have neglected to bring and, after two decades and hundreds of voyages, we still leave things behind. Additionally, although it sounds obvious, do not be influenced by the current temperature at home when selecting clothing for a distant cruise. Remembering, for example, to pack sweaters and goose-down jackets for Alaska's Glacier Bay in the sweltering humidity of New York in July requires prescient determination.

And for that awful afternoon at the end of your cruise when possessions must be urged back into suitcases, a couple of helpful pointers. Each half of a couple should pack separately, not together; you will find that the average cabin's dimensions do not harmoniously accommodate a twosome's repeated logistical shifts between bureau, closet and suitcase. Once suitcases have been packed and labeled, prior to their being deposited outside in the cabin corridor for pickup, stow them temporarily out of the way in the bathroom shower but make sure it is dry. Of course, the only compensation about vacating your cabin is that everything must be packed; not one choice need be made.

Herewith a suggested wardrobe for Nonpax, incorporating an overview of 7-14 days' cruising expectations. By day, whether on board or ashore, you can wear almost anything that you might wear at home over a weekend: Jeans, shorts, slacks, skirts and blouses for the ladies, and jeans and/or shorts or slacks for the gentlemen and, always, for both sexes, track suits. What is described in the trade loosely as leisure clothing seems endemic to today's cruise passengers, particularly senior ones. Little old ladies who, a century ago, would have strolled the decks in shirt-waist dresses, sensible shoes and straw hats, now appear togged out in vibrant nylon track suits and sometimes more vibrant sneakers.

Another absolute certainty about passengers and their clothing is that all will stock up on logo cruisewear purchased on the ship. Logo clothing from the vessel or company is obtainable only on board, in shops owned and operated by the line. In fact, casual clothing adorned with the company's or ship's logo represents a huge revenue source for the line as well as a vital piece of "I-was-there" one-upmanship for their passengers. Everything from T-shirts, caps, sweaters, sweatshirts, jackets, trousers, socks and parkas, emblazoned with the line's logo or ship's name, is available in quantity and multiple sizes.

Once they have stocked up on ship-tagged clothing, passengers add to their collection by buying T-shirts in consecutive ports, to show they have been there as well. You will probably buy so many additional cruise garments of one kind or another that I recommend you pack inside one of your suitcases a folded soft suitcase to accommodate the inevitable overage when flying home. But never fear, if you forget to do that, the on-board shopkeepers will be delighted to sell you one instead.

An on-board shopping phenomenon that never ceases to amaze is the extraordinary amount of goods of all kinds that are snapped up from shipboard's improvised market stalls. Well aware of this passenger predilection, the ship's shopkeepers devise open-air marketplaces. Every sea day is market day as tables in front of the shops are heaped with merchandise of all kinds. Never mind that passenger circulation is severely constricted, that tables laden with a tangle of fought-over T-shirts look sloppy, that the goods are often shopworn or of dubious quality. During discontinued or reduced-price clothing sales, those impromptu stalls are surrounded by a veritable feeding frenzy as lady passengers three-deep paw through the goods.

Clearly, this is no pastime for husbands; baffled and exhausted, the sensible ones retire for coffee nearby until the hubbub subsides. One day, clothing will be featured, on another bargain wristwatches or costume jewelry will be arrayed for inspection. But the change of goods makes little difference; whatever is offered, passengers in search of bargains besiege the tables, unable to resist. Despite the vaunted elegance decorating the inside of the shops in newbuilding construction, in truth, aboard today's mass market cruise ships, it is the Fileniesque furor *outside* the shops, among those irresistible market stalls, that compels most passenger attention.

As regards dress to be worn throughout your day at sea, almost anything goes. In fact, anything goes everywhere these days. I am writing these words on the ground floor of my Manhattan brownstone and through the large, distracting window immediately to my right, a constant *paseo* of contemporary passersby serves as invaluable insight into what I must describe as today's fashion Babel.

A young woman has just strolled by, wearing atop her long hair a soft wool hat trimmed with satin ribbon that her great grandmother might well have worn aboard ADRIATIC back at the turn of the century. Completing the bottom of her ensemble were sturdy Doc Martins. The body in between sported stone-washed carpenter's overalls while her neck and shoulders were encased in a frilly, peach-colored camisole.

Contemporary fashion thrives on selective anarchy; all bets are

Throughout a QUEEN ELIZABETH 2 crossing, it is understood that black tie is *de rigeur* every night save the first and last. *Barry M. Winiker*

off, all rules broken. Mix and match everything—denim with silk, brocade with leather, boots with boas; it does not seem to matter. As on Manhattan streets, as on board ship or, indeed, as everywhere in America: anything goes. Overall, two indestructible sartorial staples rule: the enshrouding T-shirt and the oft-reversed baseball cap, America's—and by extension—the world's daily *couture de choix*. Liberating perhaps but I still lament the days when we dressed carefully to go anywhere, especially embarking aboard a ship on which one would, as matter of course, dress for dinner each night.

For passengers entering the dining room, all vessels but one mandate graduated dress codes. The exception is, appropriately,

QUEEN ELIZABETH 2, the last ocean liner left in service. During crossings on that distinctive Cunarder, passengers dress in black tie for dinner every night as they did in the old days; no announcements are made, *one just dresses*.

During warm-weather cruises away from the North Atlantic, QUEEN ELIZABETH 2's regime is relaxed to conform with cruising's universal dress codes. (Although "codes" sound forbidding, do not be alarmed; they are often violated and completely unenforceable.) On every daily program that appears beneath your cabin door, the recommended code for that evening's meal will be prominently displayed.

The lowest common sartorial denominator is "casual" and casual it certainly is. Passengers come in to dine on those evenings in clothes rather similar to what they have been wearing all day, save for shorts or tank tops. The next step up, a median dress code called "informal," recommends neckties and jackets—either a suit or sports jacket or blazer—for the men and dress, skirt and blouse or pant suit for the ladies. (As a matter of conscience, training or I am not sure what, I always wear a jacket and tie to dinner, whatever the code. Few of my fellow passengers do.)

The supreme clothing mandate is "formal" and means, for gentlemen, either a tuxedo (which the French call *le smoking* but I prefer to call dinner jacket), dark suit or blazer. Ladies need no guidelines for these occasions and invariably take the opportunity, especially for the first of a seven-day cruise's two formal nights, to pull out all the *couture* stops. They have their hair done and wear their best and brightest. (Urgent note to Newpax: If your hair requires professional attention, be sure to book an appointment for the day of each formal night with one of the ship's hairdressers the moment you embark; there is not a moment to be lost.)

The first formal night is known throughout the world's cruis-

Aboard ROTTERDAM, Captain W. van der Noordt introduces his officers at the Captain's Cocktail Party.
Barry M. Winiker

ing fleets as the Captain's Welcome Aboard cocktail party. The entire passenger body or, if there are two, each sitting (see Glossary) gathers for complimentary drinks before dinner while the master introduces his senior officers. (Newpax, pray avoid what may seem a tempting jest of asking the captain if all his officers are present, who is driving the ship? It is a tiresome wheeze at which they have winced for years.) The party concludes with the master's brief speech of welcome before you descend to dine.

Within the forbidding strictures of our unisexual age, is it permissible to suggest that women enjoy dressing up more than men? I hope so for surely it is true. Alone throughout the animal world, the genus *Peregrinator Americanus* (for which read American male passenger) relinquishes pride of plumage to its distaff partner; the males of every other genus, whether peacock, cardinal, bird of paradise or lion, are equipped by nature with finer adornment to create a more imposing appearance.

But not, alas, aboard cruise ships. How many husbands—Oldpax, Newpax, Nonpax alike—when juggling luggage priorities for an upcoming cruise, will ponder the necessity of packing their dinner jacket? Too many, I fear; it is a reluctance I cannot share.

A dinner jacket in your cabin closet means that for two of seven nights, you will be appropriately dressed. And a shortage of suitcase space is no excuse. A dinner jacket takes up no more room than a suit and surely a couple of dress shirts among so many others is not a difficulty.

Sometimes, I have the impression that too many men feel that a dinner jacket is uncomfortable, that even a necktie, let alone a black bow tie, is perceived as impinging on their sense of independence, rather as though abrogating their right to bear arms. I'm here to relax, the reasoning goes; why should I dress up? One ominous relaxation has even been promulgated aboard the upscale vessels of SilverSea Cruises, a reduction in the number of formal evenings.

Some random remembrances about shipboard formal dress demand inclusion. Mary once found herself next to a honeymooning groom aboard NORWAY who confessed without a trace of embarrassment: "I've worn a tie three times in my life—once when my pappy died, yesterday at my wedding and now tonight." If a necktie was that alien to him, we can but admire his relenting on our behalf.

Then again, how many times have I seen shipboard couples who, having successfully donned festive evening dress, reappear later that evening garbed for the beach? On one recent world cruise, the passenger-load was restricted to an obviously experienced and well-heeled clientele, because all had been obliged to buy the entire cruise rather than merely a segment. The bar was thronged before the second sitting with elegantly dressed couples awaiting the dinner hour. In their midst, perched defiantly on bar stools, as though in their neighborhood tavern watching a televised double-header, was a first-sitting couple who had obviously shucked their formal clothes in favor of cut-off blue jeans, tank tops and sandals. It made for a bizarre, Arbusian spectacle, that scruffy duo juxtaposed against their appropriately dressed fellows.

Though companies are disinclined to nudge their clientele in the matter of dress or behavior, occasionally individual crew members take it on themselves. We used to sail on Royal Viking ships with a doughty Danish hostess called Yana Dunn. Yana was fiercely protective of her vessel's upscale sheen, famous for pursuing ladies down the corridor, remonstrating cogently that curlers, even concealed beneath a scarf, were not acceptable public attire "aboard my ship." Bravo, Yana, we need more arbiters with your determination and dedication. But shipboard vigilantism of that kind is rare. Most cruise staff these days would never dare reprimand a passenger for any aberration of dress, let alone decorum.

Back in the 1920s, on board the liners, American undergraduates sailing for Europe down in Tourist Third Cabin who had packed a dinner jacket were frequently sought out by the Chief Purser as suitable dancing partners for young ladies in first class. For several evenings during the crossing, those fortunate and properly attired young men would be welcomed in first class and could establish liaisons with otherwise unattainable girls, all because they had with them that essential shipboard requisite.

Gentlemen, my urgent recommendation, pack that dinner jacket and wear it with *brio*. Its presence on board and on your person will ensure your full and appropriate participation—along

Black tie and dressiest dresses reign aboard REGAL PRINCESS on the eve of her christening. *Barry M. Winiker*

with your wife's, the master's and officers' and even the dining room waiters'—in a memorable shipboard occasion. The entire vessel, its crew and its passengers sparkle on formal nights and gentlemen wearing anything other than black tie will, despite cruising's notorious one-class democracy, be relegated to second class. You will stand out as either indifferent or inexperienced; in short, you will not belong.

Am I flogging a dead horse? I think not, for one of the durable rituals of formal nights is that the ship's photographers do such a brisk trade in—what else?—formal portraits. Dozens of couples in their best attire queue up patiently before and after dinner to submit to the cameraman's scrutiny. On the following day, along the racks where photographs are put out for display, dozens of oversize prints of solemn portraits eclipse the smaller and suddenly frivolous candids by a long margin. Which leads me to believe that most shipboard couples not only enjoy dressing up, they like to memorialize the event as well.

Having addressed myself so determinedly to the gentlemen on the subject of what to pack, perhaps I should let the ladies have the last word. I started this chapter with an epigraph on the subject of clothing worn on the old steamships that cruised around the globe. To give you a flavor of the contents of those ancient wardrobe trunks, I will close this chapter with a few excerpts from Esther Boyer's chatty advice circa 1934:

". . . The summer clothes for the last two years have been ideal for tropical climes. Among them, in the sports line, are serviceable piques, shantungs, linens and other such materials in a wide choice of colors . . .

". . . Try to include one or two cotton evening gowns if possible, of charming organdie, or swiss, or embroidery, or handkerchief linen . . . If you want to know a secret, everyone envies the woman who looks as fresh as a daisy . . .

"Hats could well be confined to straw or light colored felts . . .

"If you are 'beach-minded' of course you will want to bring something in the smartest new pyjamas for the sun deck . . ."

Poor Esther Boyer, how could she have guessed what would happen to passenger clothes' sense seven decades later?

CHAPTER V

Embark and Explore

A ship is an island . . . inhabited yet mysteriously unexplored,
self-centered, secretive, wonderful, unique. Situated against a
sunset horizon or towering white-topped above a quayside,
ablaze with lights or gay with flags, it seems cut off in time
as well as space—a presence whose scale is impossible to grasp,
and whose indifference to admiration is as maddening as a cat's.

—Sir Hugh Casson

Having just recovered from five days on the QE2, *I have decided*
that prolonged luxury is not for me. There is a limit to the pleasure
I can extract from being spoilt. If everything is first-rate,
then nothing is a treat, and I begin to feel guilty that I have done
nothing to earn all this lavishness; it far exceeds my deserts.

—Nigel Nicolson

Bed, oh bed, oh bed,
Delicious bed,
That heaven on earth
To the weary head.

—Thomas S. Hood

Once your bus or taxi has left the clutter of the airport and buzzed along a length of thruway, you will arrive at the environs of the docks. And there, suddenly and rewardingly, is your vessel alongside. Regardless how many times I have first spied my ship, even though an old friend, a frisson of pleasurable anticipation colors the encounter. After all these years, the seductive apparition of a prospective ship still compels. For this is one of humanity's most exciting conveyances, fresh in from the sea, re-provisioning while awaiting her new passenger-load.

Although it would be presumptive to try and improve on his pungent epigraph reproduced above, perhaps Sir Hugh Casson would consent to an extension of that feline imagery—the moored ship as caged jungle creature, less "maddening" than merely restless. A ship confined to a pier seems a creature held against its will, tethered but yearning to shuck its bonds and return to the sea wilds where it belongs. Small wonder that this image leaps to mind for every design element of your cruise ship conveys an impression of motion and speed—the slope and flare of the bow, a long length of muscular flank, the coiled haunches aft and the funnel's dashing rake. She and all her sisters bide their time in port impatiently, ready to resume their forward momentum.

On the other hand, you might equate that pier-side vision with a castle—part Oz, part fortress concealing a promise of enchantment. That towering edifice comes complete with rampart of a hull, hawsered buttresses, a drawbridged gangway spanning its protective moat and, high atop, crenelated crystal battlements festooned with flags. Although it rarely happens these days, embarkation after dark conveys its own special resonance. An observer once characterized nocturnal AQUITANIA alongside her Southampton pier as a giant steel beehive, aglitter with chinks of

A magical moment inaugurates every cruise: ROYAL VIKING SKY starts moving away from her New York dock. Note the contrasting body language of those serenely on board and those rushing enviously along the pier.
Barry M. Winiker

light that, spilling through a multitude of glazed perforations, betrayed the inviting buzz of life inside.

You are to be welcomed within those unscalable steel walls, among the privileged of the port to gain admission. Every facet of on-board life as well as every destination at which she will call have been arranged with your interest and amusement in mind. From the experienced master on the bridge to the greenest busboy in the dining room, a crew of many hundreds has been recruited and trained to convey you along an incomparably indolent voyage.

In that regard, the passenger ship is unique; neither freighter, container ship, tanker nor warship, she is loaded with that most rarified cargo of all, a seagoing community whose welfare, safety and enjoyment constitute the vessel's sole preoccupation. The privileged sanctity of a passenger ship is never brought home to me more forcefully than when approaching Panama's legendary canal. Dozens of ships lie patiently at anchor in the Cristóbal roads, waiting their turn for admission into the locks. But our cruise ship, bound on a fixed and time-sensitive itinerary, is a privileged candidate; we glide to the head of the queue to begin our magical ascent at once.

And here on the pier, there can be no more exhilarating moment than embarkation. Travel from home achieved, you stand on your cruise's threshold, with every one of those long anticipated, sea-going days before you. The preceding passenger-load has disembarked that morning and after a brief noontime hiatus, the vessel is ready to welcome her next onslaught of clients.

But while the ship waits, you must wait too, completing a succession of nagging pier-side formalities: Tickets must be submitted, examined and checked against the vessel's manifest, passports have to be inspected, on-board credit arranged and perhaps some immigration forms filled out. But the paper cyclone does subside and, clutching a precious boarding pass, you proceed to the gangway.

There, two further delays intrude. Hand luggage must be scrutinized and X-rayed and pockets emptied before passage through that electronic arch. (Why am I always encumbered with so many metallic bits and pieces?) Then, final hurdle, embarking passengers stop for one of the vessel's ubiquitous photographers, posing for an initial shipboard candid that too often betrays only the rumpled, jet-lagged dishabille of flight, tempered by game smiles. I have always felt that cruise lines should pair those harried embarkation mug shots with serene disembarkation portraits, thereby validating shipboard's tonic effect.

Now, at last, you are cleared. Abandoning shore for ship, you stride eagerly into the belly of the beast, ready to absorb a host of novel delights. The pampering begins just inside the hull as you willingly surrender hand luggage to a solicitous, white-gloved steward who will conduct you to your deck, corridor and cabin. The door is open and inside, you will find in actuality the efficient space first envisioned in miniature on a deck plan months earlier.

Your first response? That it probably seems smaller—much smaller—than anticipated. But ignore the temptation to bolt. Years ago, in another life, I was a production stage manager on Broadway. Whenever a play went out of town for its tryout tour, my least favorite chore was making advance hotel bookings for the company. Actors are notoriously fragile in new surroundings and I always dreaded the moment when, dazed by an early morning trek from, say, Philadelphia to Boston, the ennui of a jolting train, the hugger-mugger of South Station and the struggle with suitcases, the company arrived at my recommended hotel primed for complaint. Everyone found fault with either the size of their room, its price, its location, the slightest intrusive noise, the ambience, the temperature—you name it. In short, the hotel was terrible and they insisted on my immediately finding them another.

To counter that hotel angst, I had a hard-and-fast rule—spend one night here and see me tomorrow. Predictably, by next morning, every complaint had evaporated and the company was again at peace. So too, cabins grow on one and I have never occupied a shipboard accommodation that, however disappointing initially, did not metamorphose into a comfortable no less than comforting seagoing home. I remember one initially unsettling accommodation aboard NORWAY. Cabin I-34, forward on International Deck, was a cramped inside double with archaic upper and lower berths that reduced poor Mary to tears when we first opened the door. But once unpacked and ensconced, we adjusted quite happily.

In fact, adapting happily to your cabin is mandatory because changing to another is not merely discouraged, it remains well nigh impossible. We live today within a computerized regime as unforgiving as a logic board. Aboard ship, plastic cabin keys often triple as charge card and boarding pass as well; hence, exchanging one's domicile and its key for another derails a complex train of interlocking digitalia. In fact, your cabin assignment is no longer made on board but was determined by a computer-assisted berthing officer months earlier at company headquarters. Changes, save for flood or short circuit, are not tolerated. On board every cruise ship in the world, there is a sign bolted firmly to the purser's desk, announcing that the vessel is sold out and that cabin changes are impossible. That sign remains in place even when the vessel is patently half-full.

It was simpler in the old days, when cabins were assigned at the discretion of the purser. Aboard STELLA POLARIS, that popular Norwegian cruise yacht that first sailed in the 1920s, the purser had an ingenious trick of keeping one cabin purposely empty. Inevitably, bright and early on the first sea day, the first of a succession of passenger couples would knock at his office door. Their cabin, they complained, was too crowded, too noisy, too near the bow, too near the stern, too hot, too cold, too light, too dark—the litany of cabin grievances available to a determined passenger migrant is as endless as it is predictable. In short, the couple insisted they be moved elsewhere.

The purser was all smiles. "I have just the right cabin for you," he beamed and move them he did. What they never realized was that their vacated cabin instantly became the purser's new "empty cabin," in readiness for the next malcontents. So throughout the voyage's first week, the purser played a deft game of musical cabins. All those relocated passengers were quite happy and, astonishingly, not one ever complained again, contentedly accommodated within quarters their predecessors had pronounced untenable.

I am sometimes asked: What is the most preferable location within the hull for passengers to request their cabin? If there's a possibly rough crossing in prospect, then low down amidships makes sense. But in the Caribbean, where waters stay smooth, it makes little difference—one end of the ship is as good as the other and deck height remains immaterial. In point of fact, after years of sailing, I have concluded that every cabin on board every ship, wherever located, boasts some kind of adjacency advantage, either near the dining room, near the purser's desk or near the library. Then again, after an exhausting day ashore, a lower deck location convenient to the gangway obviates the need to climb stairs or wait for an elevator. But, by the same token, high in the ship is conveniently near pool, lido and outer decks.

In truth, though your median cabin may not necessarily be luxurious, it is ingenious. And given that you will enjoy a seagoing tenancy within it for a week or more, extraordinary attention has been paid to every aspect of its comfort and convenience. All boast their own bathroom, tucked into one of the inboard corners, small, perhaps, but perfectly adequate. Its modest dimensions make sound spatial sense, for the tradeoff of a larger bathroom would be a smaller cabin. Unless you have invested heavily in the most splendid cabin high atop the ship, your bathroom will be equipped with a shower rather than a tub.

All cabin bathrooms on board were made in a factory, preassembled as huge boxes for delivery to the shipyard and installation within the hull. Everything save a damp passenger was included inside those sanitary blocks, as naval architects call them—soap dish, towel rail, toilet paper holder, shelves, cupboards and a slot for a box of Kleenex. Be warned that aboard every modern cruise ship, the flushing mechanism of the toilet works by a vacuum system which, when activated, produces a startlingly loud noise. Shipboard's vacuum toilet is a relatively recent innovation, perfected as part of a totally fresh water sewage system. As a result, corrosive salt water is no longer piped within cabin bathrooms. The only downside of shipboard's fresh water regime is that a beguiling sea water phosphorescence no longer enlivens nocturnal flushes.

At the time your vessel was under construction, an original cabin prototype was assembled and temporarily erected in a warehouse at the shipyard. Once in place and ready for inspection, it was visited extensively by teams of executives and hotel operations personnel from the prospective owner, intent on torture-testing every design feature. No shred of decor or detail escaped their scrutiny. Like unruly delinquents, they bounced on beds, opened and closed curtains to distraction, tugged at the shower curtain and wrenched every knob and pull in sight. They evaluated how comfortable the mattress, checked clearance for suitcase entry through the door as well as storage beneath the bed, made sure that every drawer and closet door worked without balking, debated the placement of shelves and hooks, tried out light levels in both bathroom and cabin and even ascertained that the dressing table finish stood up to spilled cologne or perfume. They ensured that the curtains kept daylight at bay and that neither ceiling nor reading light glared into the eyes of a passenger watching television from the bed. They shouted from outside the mockup walls to monitor noise levels that might filter from corridor or adjacent cabin and agonized over color choices for carpet, bedspread and curtain. Nothing escaped the scrutiny of those test passengers and final selection of your cabin's fittings, fabrics, fixtures and furnishings emerged only after hours of abusive study.

Incidentally, a sizeable accumulation of paper will be delivered to your cabin throughout the cruise—the daily program, shopping promotions, invitations, notes from fellow passengers, newspapers, luggage tags, customs declarations, port announcements and photographs. Traditionally, they always used to appear beneath the door; indeed, cabin sills have always served as efficient shipboard mailboxes. But recently, in an attempt to reduce noise and also as a fire precaution, the bottom of the latest cabin doors are lined with a rubber gasket that makes it impossible to slip anything underneath it. So cabin deliveries are either left curled within the door handle or dropped in a special mail rack beside each door. The original practice was far superior because the faint rustle of an envelope or newspaper being slipped into the cabin insured swift acknowledgement. Sometimes, notes or deliveries linger unheeded for hours in those exterior racks.

Within an hour of your arrival on board, your cabin steward will tap at the door and make himself or herself known to you. He or she will serve as your dedicated company servant; he will clean and make up your cabin, bring you trays or drinks, replenish your ice supply, deliver and retrieve laundry or dry cleaning, turn down your bed at night—in sum, go to diligent lengths to render your sea and port days as seamlessly pleasant as possible.

Most of today's stewards are recruited from third-world countries, young men and women who know the meaning of extremely demanding work. It would be fair to say that it is the stewards' unremitting toil, whether in cabin, dining room or public room, that is responsible for the glowing patina of cleanliness and well-being that distinguishes shipboard. In addition to taking care of you and your cabin, stewards look after about a dozen others as well; their telltale trolleys, stacked with fresh linen and towels, are harbingers of concerned service on every passenger corridor.

Cabin and dining room stewards make up the largest single manpower block of every passenger vessel and are responsible for cleaning every cabin on board, those belonging to both passengers and crew. You will find that the two-way symbiosis between passenger and steward is unique to shipboard; no hotel maid, airline hostess or even bartender is privy to the same wealth of intimate detail involving your household persona. And just as you will refer automatically to "your steward," so he or she will dub you "my passenger." The captain's steward on many lines is still called the captain's tiger because, in the days when tea clippers sailed to and from the orient, he was traditionally kitted out in the most exotic and dazzling silk finery obtainable.

An increasingly large percentage of cabins aboard cruise ships are equipped with an exterior balcony, a sheltered but open-air square footage amplification that becomes your exclusive lookout. The advent of so many balconied cabins has transformed naval architecture. Nowadays, most cruise ship flanks and sterns assume a serial, checkerboard configuration, part honeycomb, part Leavenworth. Companies are determined to incorporate as many balconies into their newbuildings as possible because they provide such a munificent return over the life of the vessel; the weekly tariff for a balconied cabin is several hundred dollars higher than for one with traditional, old-fashioned portholes.

Balconies are desirable for one very sound reason. Consider the following scenario from the days of the ocean liner. Passengers walked home the length of a traditional corridor, turned down a little athwartship alleyway and approached one of several cabin doors. Those nearest the corridor were inside cabins while those farther along and adjacent to the hull plating were outside. But whether inside or outside, conventional cabins shared a design commonality. Each was, in effect, a dead end, entered as final, irrevocable destination. To return outdoors, you were obliged to retrace your steps along the alleyway and corridor and then up a flight or two of stairs before re-emerging onto an open deck. Since all of today's cabins are air-conditioned, hermetically sealed portholes further isolate you from the sea.

But equipped with a balcony, your corridor/alleyway/cabin cul-de-sac becomes a beguiling conduit, leading to a private aerie. On impulse, you can step outdoors directly from the cabin to sample the weather or, even more evocative, hear and smell the sea or inspect an imminent landfall. These perquisites remain, unquestionably, among the balcony's overriding advantages. You are no longer arbitrarily pigeonholed indoors but are, instead, within instantaneous and easy reach of outdoors.

But be warned that your lookout comes at a price: It is a chronic time-waster. Those with balconies tend not only to shun the promenade deck but also to linger at their own railing, habitually late for drinks or dinner because the hypnotic ambience of their superstructural perch is so captivating. Pacific sunsets—or, conversely, sunrises—are particular villains in this regard, keeping balcony owners transfixed before their private panorama.

However beguiling balconies are for passengers, some crew members are less enthusiastic. They are the despair of the ship's engineers because open balcony doors raise havoc with air conditioning norms. Stewards must cope with torn curtains left flying

Chance encounters along the promenade deck are the lifeblood of cruising.
Barry M. Winiker

in the breeze—simultaneously open cabin and balcony doors create a tornado—while damp footprints sully the cabin carpet. Then again, litter accumulates on hundreds of wind traps flanking the ship's sides.

On a socio/architectural level, I have discovered that the increasing profusion of private balconies fragments the passenger-load. Traditionally, there have always been specifically communal moments during cruises, early-morning arrival in a new port or subsequent departure at dusk. On both occasions, fellow passengers throng the promenade deck railings, shoulder-to-shoulder, sharing delighted anticipation or flushed with pleasure following adventures ashore. Conversations are struck up, impressions exchanged and new friends made. My sense is that the promenade deck, though traditionally an arena of exercise or reflection, fulfills its most invaluable shipboard function as a cordial meeting ground, scene of countless impulsive encounters. Shipboard acquaintances initiated along promenade deck railings often blossom into friendship for the duration of the cruise or even thereafter.

But the increasing availability of balconied cabins has curtailed much of that irreplaceable passenger interaction. When the ship sails out of port, those without balconies gather, as they always have, along the promenade deck. But their ranks are thinned because too many of their fellows are ensconced instead atop isolated superstructure perches like starlings on a wire. As a result, a subtle, discriminatory shipboard schism has been established, separating more affluent passengers from their fellows and hence eroding contemporary cruising's one-class ethos.

Perhaps this is the moment to try and unravel the historic intricacies of shipboard classes because they relate, so specifically, to the nature of the cabin in which you will find yourself. Traditionally, throughout decades of ocean liner travel, passengers crossing the Atlantic or the Pacific were segregated within rigid class enclaves. As a matter of course, naval architects sub-divided ocean liner decks and interiors into either two, three or occasionally four shipboard classes. Each was assigned its own dining room, lounge, library, purser's square and promenade; and the size and splendor of every cabin varied in accordance with the class in which it was located. Moreover, when passengers disembarked in Liverpool, Southampton or Le Havre to board boat trains for the ride up to London or Paris, they entered first or second class carriages, extending the ocean liner's class divisions throughout the railed portion of their crossing as well.

Yet despite that pervasive shipboard norm, the very same passengers embarked on cruises to find that traditional class barriers had been obliterated. Since the very beginning, cruise ships without exception have *always* featured a single class only. In retrospect, it seems astonishing that a venerable company like Cunard, in the business of transporting segregated passengers across the Atlantic aboard, for instance, staid old AQUITANIA, would then lump them all together in one ship-wide class while the same vessel idled in the Caribbean or the Mediterranean. More to the point, why did their class-imprinted clients accept that abrupt democratization?

The answer, of course, is that transatlantic liners catered to a broad sociological spectrum. Their contrasting layers of deck were filled with a polyglot clientele so economically diverse that any thought of shipboard homogeneity was denied. Whereas first class banker might have mingled, albeit uneasily, with the salesman of the second, neither would have dreamed of rubbing elbows with the hordes thronging the lowest decks. The contrasting nature of the ocean liner traffic, from upper deck high-born to berthing compartment hoi polloi, made segregation by class inevitable.

However, it was perceived that passengers embarking for an adventurous cruise could be treated differently. They were not obliged to visit the Holy Land or North Cape; they were there by choice. Cruise clients then and now share a congenial common interest, on board because they *wish to be*, not because they *have to be*. Of course, there was another good reason that argued persuasively for making cruises one class. Whereas ocean liner passengers disembarked only at their destination, the very nature of cruising dictated several consecutive disembarkations en route, almost always by tender. And tendering cruise passengers ashore while observing class distinctions would have proved logistically challenging.

Today, apart from the balcony differential discussed above, the sole legacy of class barriers aboard "one-class" ships is the option of booking more expensive and hence more splendid cabins. Throughout the modern cruise ship, occupants of every level of accommodation—whether a suite with a balcony or a humble inside cabin—are rewarded with square footage and splendor pegged unerringly to the price they have paid for their passage. Indeed, the sole remaining bastion of shipboard privilege today revolves around the cabin. Within your shipboard home, you may be king but everywhere else, you revert to commoner, enjoying no special privileges whatsoever.

Earlier, I suggested that the ship's gangway served as your cruise threshold. Equally important is the on-board threshold beneath your cabin door. Once exiting across it, forsaking your private quarters, you move into strictly one-class territory among a host of passenger equals, sharing identical food, entertainment and perquisites regardless of how rarified your living quarters.

Let me make one final observation about this complex subject. Shipboard's ancient class system still persists but in a subtle and largely unremarked way. Though one-class cruising is touted as the industry norm, vestigial first class adherents have merely jumped ship, rewarding their patronage to smaller, more refined vessels of other lines. The socio/cultural gulf distinguishing first from tourist class aboard ocean liners is little different from the contrasting tastes and expectations separating megaship Newpax ploughing around the Caribbean from hidebound Oldpax embarked for three months circumnavigating the globe. In that sense, shipboard classes remain stubbornly in place, although in a configuration that old-line pursers might never have guessed. Nowadays, first and tourist classes are separated not by layers of deck but miles of ocean instead.

Once your luggage has been delivered, you will probably want to take a moment or two to start unpacking. If you can find room in your suitcases, I recommend that you bring a few personal items as cabin decoration, framed photographs or any reminders of home. When the grand old CARONIA used to circle the globe each winter during the 1950s, several of her most recherché clients used to

Lifeboat drill aboard CRYSTAL HARMONY. *Barry M. Winiker*

bring with them not only their own linen but paintings and even furniture as well. They were not necessarily sprucing up their quarters, only surrounding themselves with things familiar. Of course, whereas CARONIA world cruise passengers were on board for months on end, you may only be at sea for a week or two. Nevertheless, I have always found that personalizing your shipboard dwelling is rewarding. Additionally, your steward will be delighted to share photographic glimpses of your family and home. Crewmen of every nationality have in common an abiding affection for children, poignant reminders of homes and families they see too infrequently.

Invariably, just as you decide to leave your cabin to explore the ship, a disembodied voice from the bridge will announce that a lifeboat drill is about to take place. This is a standard cruising ritual that, under maritime law, must take place within 24 hours of embarkation. It is a brief but necessary exercise and what better time to participate than now. You will find lifejackets either set out on the beds or on the top or bottom shelf of the cabin closet. On the back of the cabin door, your lifeboat number is posted (even ones are always hung on the port side, the odd to starboard), the location of an interior mustering station and the most expeditious route to both. Some companies call the roll at lifeboat drills; others rely on your good sense to attend. For many years, these drills were treated as something of a lark and it was common for shipboard photographers to prowl the promenade decks, snapping candids of lifejacketed clients. But I always felt that trivializing what is in effect a serious and instructive occasion was wrong and I am pleased to note that the practice has ceased. You will either be assembled on an open promenade deck next to your lifeboat or in one of several public room mustering stations. The Dutch favor the outdoor option and even lower a lifeboat to embarkation level so that passengers can inspect the interior. Whether outdoors or in, the captain will deliver a short talk about shipboard safety over the ship's speaker system and members of the crew will demonstrate the correct way to tie on your lifejacket.

Once dismissed from the drill, now is the moment to re-stow your lifejackets in the cabin and explore the rest of the vessel. Having completed lifeboat drill, you will already have seen either the promenade deck or a public room; however, more on-deck and 'tween deck awaits. Hedonists should repair at once to the beauty salon to make that hair appointment for the afternoon of the captain's welcome aboard (already recommended) while gourmands all should hasten to the dining room to discuss their table seating with the maître d'hôtel.

No more important errand awaits the newly embarked passenger. As our ensuing chapter will describe in detail, shipboard meals are perceived by the line as pivotal to enjoyment of your voyage.

CHAPTER VI

To Table

Cooking means comfort, and pleasure, and good health, and good temper, and I don't know what else besides—why it's everything, is cooking. All the good in the world has always been done after a good dinner.

—Isabella Beaton, *Beaton's Book of Household Management*

Remember, never try to eat anything you can't lift.

—Waggish advice from an anonymous North Atlantic chief steward

Often, when I roam about one of today's megaships, with its extensive deckscapes and suites of public rooms, I cannot help but think back to the modest dimensions of the vessels on which our forebears sailed during the early nineteenth century. Under way, passengers aboard those earliest liners had at their disposal only three possible venues: The claustrophobic, sometimes damp isolation of their cabins, moist open decks cluttered with rigging for the sails or gathering together in what was called the dining saloon.

This last was that era's great public room, the only on-board space in which all the vessel's occupants could assemble at one time; as a result, it remained in almost constant use. To start with, three meals a day and a sizable allotment of spirits were consumed therein. And once stewards had replaced the tables' oilcloth with green baize, the dining saloon morphed instantly into shipboard lounge, the ship's sole arena for much earnest palaver, a great deal of distracted reading, sing-songs or amateur theatricals and, throughout long creaking nights, endless sessions of whist. Once each week on the Sabbath, saloon segued into church as the master conducted divine services from a flag-draped head table.

Small wonder that this gathering place assumed overwhelmingly symbolic importance, shipboard focus of sustenance, warmth, light and, perhaps most important of all, companionship. Enforced residence within a vessel pitching and tossing about the North Atlantic was a real test of the passenger spirit. In contrast with the unfettered ease of life aboard today's cruise ships, conditions aboard nineteenth century steamers were primitive. When the weather misbehaved—and it often did—the tenor of life below decks ranged from nervous-making to terrifying. As waves battered the hull and superstructure, jarring motion and noise engendered a sense of fearful vulnerability.

Not surprisingly, passengers confined below forsook their cabins in search of kindred spirits. The solace they sought could be found only in the dining saloon, where the prospect of food was almost of less importance than the prospect of communion with others. Thrice daily, the ritual of breaking bread with their fellows guaranteed cherished conviviality, food for the soul as much as for the stomach.

How, one might ask, does this ancient predilection relate to life aboard today's vessels? The answer is simple: The mystique of shipboard dining remains just as potent a wellspring of passenger

Whether in IMPERATOR's dining saloon of 1913 or the elegant Manhattan dining room aboard today's MERCURY, more than food nourishes passengers at shipboard tables. *Author's Collection* and *Barry M. Winiker*

preoccupation. Although few if any passengers aboard today's cruise ships may be uneasy or frightened, many are lonely and the business of gathering for meals remains freighted with potent, psychological significance.

Moreover, a ship's dining room has always fulfilled another vital function, as a social arena where you can inspect and evaluate your fellow passengers. Occupants of any conveyance going anywhere have always exhibited a proprietary concern for—no less than curiosity about—those sharing their journey. I think this is a peculiarly American trait, that we tend to be gregarious for sound historical reasons. Early stagecoach or riverboat passengers, wending their way across a potentially hostile wilderness, were anxious to ascertain the mettle of those traveling with them. In the event of sudden attack, storm or emergency of any kind, they liked knowing precisely on whom they could count. Today's contrasting regional characteristics reflect that early predisposition. Westerners to this day are more open and more likely to talk with strangers, bonhomie that insular, parochial easterners sometimes find difficult. Aboard a cruise ship, just as on an ocean liner, it is at the dining table that you can, at your leisure, get to know your fellow passengers.

One of the most crucial aspects of cruise ship dining is with whom and how many one sits and at what kind of table. The effort of assigning passengers to the right table is what ages maîtres d'hôtel. These are supremely accomplished company servants, men who have risen steadily up through the catering ranks from lowly commis (or assistant) waiter to full waiter to dining room captain to the top of their profession as maîtres d'hôtel. But however challenging their past careers, whatever trials they once endured with overladen trays, harsh superiors, finicky passengers or the sticky remnants of a storm-wracked dining table, nothing from that testing apprenticeship fully prepares them for the angst, irritation and diplomacy involved in trying to seat passengers in the dining room.

Eating meals aboard ship should be simple, right? It used to be. A hundred years ago, passengers in every dining saloon faced one another along both sides of boarding-house tables, perched either on benches or, subsequently, individual cast-iron swivel chairs bolted to the deck. The only passenger couples' choice was the location of two seats along a selection of identically long tables. Today, every ship's dining room, whether aboard a small yacht-like vessel or within a megaship's cavernous chamber, is furnished with a mixture of tables: There are eights—either round or rectangular—sixes, fours and, in chronic short supply, tables for two, known in the trade as deuces.

To illustrate the potential hazards of dining table assignments, herewith a worst-case scenario. Austrian Arnold Deutschl once served as a supremely accomplished and charming maître d' with the Royal Viking Line in the 1980s. He had to cope with a host of demanding repeat passengers, all of them aggressively articulate about where they wanted to sit and with whom.

At the start of one longish cruise, old friends of Arnold's, an embarking couple from San Francisco—let us call them the Smiths—had been promised a table for two at a window by the head office. But after that first frenetic evening, once 750 Royal Viking diehards had unleashed their demands, it emerged that Mr. and Mrs. Smith's promised deuce would not—*could* not—be anywhere near a window.

Refusing to accept the inevitable, infuriated Mr. Smith cajoled, argued, blustered and stormed but to no avail. He even tried calling San Francisco to overrule the shipboard decision. Finally, by way of underscoring his displeasure, he decided never to address poor Arnold again, not only throughout that cruise but many more to follow. Now, admittedly, this unsavory episode can be viewed as an isolated anomaly, an arrogant passenger of surpassing rudeness who should have known better. Nevertheless, that unfortunate Deutschl/Smith imbroglio also serves to illustrate the relentless lengths to which some will go to bludgeon a maître d'hôtel into complying with their sometimes unrealistic dining vision.

But before badgering your maître d'hôtel about a preferred table, you must first decide which sitting you prefer. Double sittings are necessary because most dining rooms can accommodate only half the passenger-load at a time. All regular shipboard meals are served twice in what are called two consecutive sittings. The food at both sittings is identical; only the times vary. The first (or early or main) sitting for dinner usually begins at 6 p.m. while the second (or late) sitting starts at 8. Before you opt for one or the other, be aware that the corollary of early lunch and dinner is early breakfast as well, obliging you to be at your dining room table no later than 7:30 every morning.

Although making shipboard generalizations can be dangerous, I have found that for the most part, older and/or less sophisticated passengers book first sitting because they tend to retire and hence rise earlier. Incidentally, companies often try to steer passengers to more sparsely attended sittings by using marketing strategy in naming them. Identifying first sitting as "Main Sitting" conveys the subliminal message that it remains the preferred selection while use of the term "Late Sitting" carries with it the implication that it may be somehow tardy or unreliable.

Choosing a sitting is easy and the cruise line's head office will assign you to the one you request months in advance of embarkation. They will also assign you to dine with what their computer has decided will be congenial tablemates. And there's the rub: No computer I have ever encountered is capable of analyzing the infinite complexities of the human condition. Mismatched fellow passengers can end up at table together, hopelessly at odds socially, psychologically or emotionally, sentenced to catering purgatory that is neither convivial nor rewarding in any way.

Short of equipping every dining room exclusively with tables for two, the potential for dining room disappointment is regrettably unavoidable. One sensible suggestion is to request an eight-seater rather than a four; among six dining companions, it is statistically more likely that a glimmer of compatibility may emerge. Always request a round rather than rectangular eight-seater because liberating cross-table chatter is the norm rather than confinement within a bleak corner.

What can be done if the situation seems hopeless? It depends entirely on you. You can either try making the best of it, enduring unsuitable, incompatible or irritating table companions throughout the cruise or you can approach the maître d'hôtel and request reassignment elsewhere. Of course, you could be leaping from frying pan into fire; however, if Table A seems really intolerable, moving to Table B, C or even D is worth a try. One cardinal rule is to make your move as soon as possible; the longer you wait, the harder it becomes. Over the first two days of the cruise, passengers in search of soulmates as tablemates keep the dining room in a kind of turmoil. By the third night, things tend to gel; the game of musical chairs is over and the maître d'hôtel, having shuffled passengers and shortened his eraser for the last time (until the next cruise), can relax, his most onerous chore once again behind him.

Mind you, imperfect as computers may be, maîtres d'hôtel often fare no better. An experienced Italian maître d' once suggested that his sole criterion for insuring passenger congeniality was age; he routinely assigned passengers to tables occupied by obvious contemporaries. In so doing, he often filled an entire eight with widows, an assignment that many of those involuntary singles perceived as an arguable slight.

But perhaps he was close to the truth; in general, mingling passengers of the same age makes sense. Conversely, combining markedly different age groups can prove catastrophic. I have never forgotten the attractive young lady who complained heatedly to me that she dined each evening with half a dozen reactionary septuagenarians whose entire conversation was devoted to bitter recriminations "about dead politicians I've never heard of." Yet, another age disparity aboard a Carnival ship produced positively euphoric results. The computer had placed an adolescent male at a table for four occupied by three elderly widows. To everyone's surprise, the arrangement worked splendidly; he amused them and they—jointly—mothered him.

By and large, your average passenger cross-section is nothing more than a microcosm of the variable human spectrum. Mary and I still recall with a shudder being assigned to a rectangular eight-seater where one half of the table never spoke to the other; a two-week's worth of meals was consumed within an adversarial chill reminiscent of East and West Berlin. It is a sad truth that anti-social or offensive behavior ashore is not miraculously cured by sea air. Some of your fellow passengers may talk too much, drop too many names or carry on *ad nauseam*, either about past cruises or perhaps their prevailing medical conditions. Others may have grating table manners or run the gamut from unconscionable prying to obdurate clannishness. And a chronic drunk always upsets any table's equilibrium.

Conversely, that great seating computer in the sky can work

The author and his wife at the conclusion of lunch at their deuce in the aftermost dining room of NORWEGIAN DREAM. *Author's Collection*

miracles. I have seen eight-seaters of four couples who enter the dining room as perfect strangers only to disembark at cruise's end lifelong friends. Moreover, their random table assignment establishes a pattern of ship-wide cohesion; the same octet sits around the pool together, goes ashore together and attends the evening shows together. At the very least, for those not accomplished at making friends, the enforced assignment of tablemates can be a godsend by way of initiating friendships, if not for life, at least for the length of the voyage. On some vessels, a selection of large tables are hosted by the ship's senior officers—the purser, the chief engineer, the staff captain, etc. Although they will only tend to be seated with you during certain evenings, you will derive interesting insights into the true life of the ship by chatting with these knowledgeable professionals.

I must confess that Mary and I make a point of requesting a table for two, for defensive reasons. Although traveling heavy, we try hard to eat light. Spending about a third of each year afloat, we have found through painful experience that ruthless caloric vigilance is mandatory. The plenitude of food aboard cruise ships is highly seductive and, in the past, we have found it devilishly easy to succumb. More than once aboard Sitmar's FAIRSEA, we fell into the terrible habit of a movable lunch, starting in the pizza parlor, then adjourning to the stern for that day's pasta offering before descending to the dining room to finish up. Although over-indulgence over one cruise need not prove fatal, the potential ballooning effect following several voyages can be frightening.

Enthusiastic consumption of good food is so contagious that, when sharing a table with six trenchermen, we tend to eat more of everything, from bread to desert. Whereas confined to a deuce of our own, intake can be reduced or at least rigidly monitored. In fact, we are inevitably the despair of dining room personnel who, because we order only two courses, feel they have somehow failed to deliver a satisfactory dining experience. As it is, we have customarily completed our frugal meal before most of our fellow passengers have tucked into their entrees. Happiness at the Maxtone-Graham household after return from the sea is some loss of weight countered by modest roulette gains.

But you should not feel in any way obligated to embrace our self-imposed, Spartan regime. You are on board to enjoy yourselves, to revel in cruising's delights and should embrace whatever gastronomic indulgences please you. As mentioned earlier, cruise ship food comes free with your ticket and Lord knows, there is plenty of it.

In my neighborhood along Manhattan's upper west side, there is a constant turnover of restaurants. Many open, few survive. I think those brave new eateries founder so regularly because the owners' first preoccupation has been with decorator rather than chef. The intrinsic value of every worthwhile restaurant is not the wallpaper but the point of view of the kitchen, just as the core business of every shipboard dining room is the galley. Although those floating caravansaries are beautifully designed and wrought, what really matters is the quality and plenitude of food that stewards deliver from the adjacent galley. Second only to the safety of their vessels, the most urgent priority shared by every cruise line is provision of good food attentively served. Inadequate or inferior food aboard a cruise ship will galvanize an instant groundswell of passenger opprobrium. Miss a port, lose some luggage or produce an inferior production show and morale survives; but offer a regime of consistently indifferent meals or surly waiters and it will rankle forever.

So, you have your table and, for better or worse, your table-mates. Over the course of your dining room tenancy on board, five staff members—one of them, alas, a ghost (about whom more in a moment)—will intersect with your dining orbit. The most important of these will be your table steward or waiter and his assistant commis waiter or busboy. Their immediate superior, the supervisory dining room captain, will put in an occasional appearance; he is one of about six in the dining room, charged with overseeing a section of tables. Periodically—but only after he has finished re-seating unhappy passengers—the boss of bosses, your maître d'hôtel, will stop by to "make nice," as they used to say at Catskill resorts, and see that you are content.

The aforementioned ghost will be, at least aboard some mass market tonnage, your sommelier or wine steward. Too many wine stewards, sad to relate, are no longer with us, victims of cruising's ubiquitous bottom line. Cost-cutting executives ashore decided several years ago to delegate the chore of selecting, fetching, uncorking and pouring wine to their already hard-pressed waiting staff. In so doing, they banished dozens of knowledgeable dining room specialists who (a) knew something about wine and (b) boasted a talent for serving it.

Although the dining room stewards are grateful for the percentage of the wine bill that rewards their efforts, their already demanding schedule is overloaded; and passenger service has suffered accordingly. On a recent cruise, I clocked the time it took Ricardo, our busboy, to complete his vintner's duties before the—presumably—paramount business of eating could begin. Once the occupants of his four tables had perused the wine list, Ricardo took their orders before disappearing to the restaurant bar. He returned with four unopened bottles. Each had to be submitted to the appropriate passenger for label inspection before Ricardo amateurishly extracted four corks and wrapped a napkin around each bottle's neck. Then, four times, an approval taste had to be proffered and a pour verdict elicited before glasses could be filled. Time elapsed? 12 minutes. Every dinner order had been taken by his superior but Ricardo, who normally would long since have raced to the galley for a tray of appetizers, was bogged down dispensing wine instead. Note to companies that have opted to do without wine stewards: It is an ill-advised, short-term economy that has seriously eroded the quality, no less than the tempo, of your on-board product. I am pleased that on some ships, at least, the sensible separation of ordering and delivering food and drink remains as it always was.

I have read that aboard Disney's two cruise ships introduced in the late 1990s, passengers migrate over the course of their voyage from one identically configured but differently decorated dining room to another; I am also delighted to learn that their table waiters migrate with them. What a sensible arrangement! For the bedrock *sine qua non* governing shipboard dining is that unique symbiosis existing between passenger and dining room steward.

The importance of that historic relationship cannot be overestimated. Just as he or she is your steward, so you are his or her passenger. Endemic to good stewarding skill is observing, absorbing and remembering the eating habits—however peculiar—of every occupant of their tables throughout both sittings of all three meals.

Shipboard breakfasts, for example, bristle with oddball preferences. Some passengers like their grapefruit untouched by the galley staff, preferring instead to dissect it themselves with a steak knife. Some relish coffee before cereal, others are extremely specific about the brewing of their tea. Some enjoy their grits served apart from their bacon and eggs, many insist on brown sugar with their cereal. One travels with his own jar of cayenne pepper, another insists on toast delivered in a rack—the list of passenger eating quirks is endless. Yet whatever the particular idiosyncrasy, a conscientious and skilled steward will, within 24 hours, have committed to memory every one of his passengers' foibles. This unique, individualized talent, impossible in a restaurant ashore, is what gives cruise ship dining room staffs their particular distinction. By the end of the cruise, your steward can practically order your meal for you.

And how he or she works on your behalf! Theirs is a non-stop ordeal repeated six times daily, seven days a week, a grueling repetitious foot race between demanding diners and the cacophony of a working galley in full swing. The waiter's dining room locus is called a side stand or service station; British stewards long ago christened it the dummy. Whatever its name, it is a bureau-sized satellite pantry, one of dozens scattered around the dining room. Within its cramped, stainless steel interior are heated plates, doilies, silver, coffee pots—all the ancillary dressing demanded for table presentation. Atop the dummy, there is scant space for the outsize trays that are your steward's conveyor of necessity.

Those laden bakelite ovals—sometimes stacked high with 24 covered entrees at a time—are either sped from galley to table or, galley-bound again, must be heaped discretely with return cargoes of uneaten food scraped into an upturned plate cover, stacks of soiled plates, a canister of used silver, all the detritus of half-consumed dinners. Receiving and dispatching these two-way deliveries requires exquisite choreography between steward and busboy, shoehorning newly arrived tray over its inverted mate that will subsequently take away the dirties.

As though that gargantuan labor alone were not sufficient, there are cardinal rules to observe: Never say no, always advise, cajole or persuade with a smile, keep up the charm, keep water glasses full, hasten hot rolls and bread from the bakery, juggle orders for post-prandial coffee or tea, never break a sweat and face the second sitting with the same enthusiasm that greeted the first. The stewards' toil is unremitting and their skilled teamwork and good cheer are a sustaining delight for passengers. Engaging factotums, brimming with good advice, buoyant pleasantry and wise counsel, they remain your staunchest shipboard allies.

If you prefer eating informally, every ship boasts a standard, built-in alternative, more often than not identified as the lido restaurant. Breakfast and luncheon are available in this cafeteria-style venue throughout a generous span of hours, regardless of your sitting. This is a good thing for passengers who like to drift in for a casual breakfast or lunch on impulse or those who have missed their dining room schedule. Lido restaurants, customarily high in the ship, are adjacent to the pool, of particular convenience to swimmers or sunbathers who are anxious for a bite of lunch but do not wish to bother changing into dry clothes for the dining room.

Traditionally, lido restaurants used to dispense meals only during daylight hours. But these days, rather than shutting down those chow lines after dark, cruise lines are gussying them up, complete with tablecloths, candles and waiter service. This nocturnal gentrification is part of contemporary shipboard's latest catering gambit, the provision of additional passenger eating spaces all over the ship; the buzzword is alternative dining.

No longer content with offering meals merely in dining room or lido, companies are determined to enlarge their gustatory horizons. Serving three meals on rigid schedule at the same table with the same companions is perceived by today's management as archaic. To bring things up to date, owners have incorporated into their latest newbuildings as many alternative restaurants as possible. Aboard GRAND PRINCESS, for example, in addition to the three regular dining rooms, there is a pizzeria, an Italian restaurant called Sabatini's, the Tex/Mex Painted Desert, a hot dog/hamburger joint and ice cream bar near the pool, and meal availability *24 hours a day* in both the Horizon Court, the vessel's lido restaurant atop the ship, or via room service delivered to your cabin. There is not a moment during every 24-hour day when you cannot enjoy a meal; that new round-the-clock meal availability has consigned that perennial cruising standby, the midnight buffet, to maritime limbo.

Creation of these additional dining facilities duplicates, in a sense, options that were commonly available aboard the great ocean liners of the 30s and 40s, eateries characterized as "extra-tariff." Aboard the two QUEENS, for example, one paid a supplementary charge (five shillings a head in the early 50s) to lunch or dine in the Verandah Grill, enjoying a day or a night out in a different venue with friends and at an hour of one's choosing. In fact, although today's alternative dining locales are ostensibly free, a minimal gratuity for the steward—usually about $3.50—is tacked onto your shipboard account for the privilege of eating there. These new dining rooms are heaven-sent facilities for officers and senior staff, enabling them to enjoy an occasional evening out, so to speak, in mid-ocean.

There is only one unfortunate downside to the proliferation of alternative restaurants: Dining room personnel is stretched thin, so thin in fact, that aboard vessels where multiple venues thrive, daytime service in the regular dining rooms suffers accordingly. All dining room breakfasts and lunches are dispensed in a mode identified in cruisespeak as open sitting. In other words, your regular table and regular steward are suddenly no longer yours; instead, as you enter the dining room, you will find that all passengers are being seated haphazardly with strangers.

What's wrong with that, you might well ask? What's wrong is that open sitting abrogates the time-honored shipboard norm of a concerned steward who has been assigned to you for the duration of the cruise, a steward whom you know and, even more important, who knows and cares about you. Anonymous waiters officiating at open-sitting tables provide perfunctory service at best. In fact, the best resolution of the open seating quagmire is to enter the dining room defensively with a group of friends; then the captain will be obliged to accommodate you *en masse* at an empty table.

Upscale, expensive cruise lines such as Sea Goddess, Seabourn and Silversea make a proud point of offering passengers permanent open sitting in their dining rooms. You drift down to dine at your leisure throughout a two-hour dining window, selecting a table wherever and with whomever you wish. Since a scrupulously observed "no tipping" regime is mandated aboard these high per diem vessels, waiters who look after a different clientele each evening have little incentive to excel; no tip is at stake. Though polished, the service, it must be added, remains curiously impersonal. However upscale the ship or ambitious the management, non-tipped waiters have little opportunity to get to know individual diners and so do not necessarily hustle on their behalf; Tuesday night's passengers will probably have decamped elsewhere by Wednesday. Of course, if you make a habit of patronizing the same table and the same steward each evening, a rapport of sorts may be established; regardless, the goad of a potential tip is denied. So paradoxically, the same problem that bedevils open-sitting lunches aboard mass-market Caribbean tonnage recurs to some extent in the dining rooms of their upscale rivals. Missing is that traditional interface between passenger and steward, the major portion of whose wages—for which read tips—depends critically on performance.

We shall try and explore all the vexing ramifications of shipboard tipping in Chapter IX. I have concluded after decades aboard ship that a steward who (a) knows you and (b) anticipates a tip at voyage's end still offers the most rewarding dining room service. And despite the open-sitting policy in vogue aboard Caribbean tonnage for breakfast and lunch, come evening, things revert happily to normal. You will be re-seated at your own table under the comforting and efficient ministration of your accustomed steward.

A final dining room insight: Near cruise's end, the penultimate or final night's meal is often described as the captain's dinner. This is a frankly manipulated evening of sentimental leave-taking and celebration. Paper hats and noisemakers are often found waiting for you at table, fomenting a kind of end-of-term, giddy hilarity throughout the dining room.

In fact, the original captain's dinners were established of necessity in the early days of transatlantic sailing packets, meals that contrasted dramatically with the light-hearted occasions we enjoy today. Long before steam drastically reduced crossing time, immigrants were required to embark aboard sailing packets with their own supplies of food. Granted access to primitive cooking facilities in a portion of the galley, they were able to prepare their own meals at vastly reduced expense.

Anticipated sailing passage to New York was approximately six weeks. However, adverse winds or storm could frequently extend the voyage, putting immigrant food reserves at risk. When too many additional days had to be spent at sea, steerage rations were often exhausted. To counter that shortfall, captains were empowered by the owners to issue additional food from company supplies among their humblest clients. So the captain's dinner, nowadays embracing a mood of frivolous celebration, originated in a very different mode, one of not only celebration but also compassion, when the master of an overdue vessel would distribute literally lifesaving nourishment.

Although it would be decades before steerage passengers boasted their own dining saloon aboard transatlantic liners, the dispensation and consumption of food to every class aboard a ship has always been inexplicably intertwined with passenger morale. It was more than hunger, more than sustenance, more even than the fashion parades aboard twentieth century ships, that compelled prompt attendance at table. Gathering for meals and enjoying the ceremony surrounding them remain at the very totemistic center of the shipboard experience. When today's cruise ship occupants flock enthusiastically into dining rooms, they are merely following in the footsteps of their ocean liner forebears.

CHAPTER VII

Evenings

After dinner, we went and persuaded the captain to let us get up another dance. We rounded up all the loafers and idlers who were glad of that species of exercise. We then went to bed after taking orangeade.

—Somerset de Chair's diary aboard a Blue Funnel liner, June 1924

Parmi les vedettes qui animent vos soirées.
(Among the stars who lend enchantment to your evenings).

—Introductory legend in glitter letters atop a signboard aboard FRANCE

Apart from very special itineraries in unrelentingly tropical waters, evening life at sea is confined almost totally to indoors. Open decks at night are, if not uninhabitable, at least ill suited for ambulatory passengers. Under way after dark, outdoors is invariably windy and moist.

Regardless, habitually deserted nocturnal decks have never quite obliterated one seemingly indestructible shipboard fantasy. Many of you will be as familiar with it as I am for it is a consistent, pictorial wish dream used by illustrators and advertisers alike, a cruising confection that, however ludicrous, remains stubbornly affixed within the media's shipboard imagination.

An elegantly dressed couple lounges at the ship's railing (invariably next to a life ring), silhouetted against the path of the moon's reflection over the sea. He is impeccably clad in tails, a white silk scarf draped languidly across his shoulders; her delicately layered organza is generously décolleté. He sometimes sports a monocle, she frequently brandishes a cigarette holder. A brace of leashed borzoi lurk at their side. Champagne glasses, filled to the brim, balance miraculously atop the rail and neither the zephyr dappling the moon river nor the ship's breeze of passage ruffles the golden pair or anything they wear; not a hair is out of place.

However seductive, that clichéd vision is flawed. Those poseurs are fantasy figures from central casting and their choice of evening venue does not reflect shipboard reality at all. After dinner aboard a cruise ship, you and your fellow passengers will be somewhere below, roaming from one public room to another. And what precise space you occupy, for how long and what you do therein is of keenest interest to the cruise line. In fact, from the very first moment of a vessel's design cycle, it remains the naval architect's paramount concern to anticipate and facilitate the variegated occupancy flows connecting public rooms. Just as the number of seats in every vessel's complement of lifeboats is of vital consequence, so too the apportionment of square feet and seats throughout public spaces remains an overwhelming design preoccupation.

In that regard, it is a curious and little-remarked fact of cruising life that there are few occasions when a ship's entire passenger load is in evidence at one time. The only two hard and fast exceptions I can think of are during lifeboat drill on the first day or on the last day when passengers, displaced from their cabins, camp temporarily in the public rooms, awaiting the summons to disembark. In between those two inescapable cruise bookends, the sight of the vessel's entire passenger-load remains elusive. Of course, there are times approaching a popular port, while tenders or gangway are being made ready, when it may *seem* that every passenger on board is pacing the deck or thronging the stairs, fretting in their anxiety to be first ashore.

But countering that herd instinct, built into the cruise ship's geography no less than its daily schedule, is a scheme of selective spatial segregation. Around the clock, an immutable passenger tidal flow surges gently and almost imperceptibly throughout the vessel. Whether they realize it or not, from the moment they board, the entire cruising clientele falls prey to this relentless lunar pull. Hence, for much of the day and night, approximately half the passenger load is rendered miraculously invisible with many public rooms mysteriously deserted.

Follow with me a typical evening's passenger prestidigitation. While first sitting is tucking into dinner, second sitting is, in effect, scattered all over the vessel. Although most are certainly napping or dressing in their cabins, others may be catching the last rays of sun, browsing in the shops, worrying at a slot machine, checking a book out of the library or enjoying a cocktail in one of the bars. Incidentally, you should be prepared for one slightly jarring aspect of shipboard sittings' overlap. It frequently happens to me. After the sun sets, as a second sitting habitué, I often descend in sweater and shorts from deck chair to cabin. I turn a corner only to find myself, painfully under-dressed, in the midst of first sitting fellow passengers all done up in their best bib and tucker, bound for the dining room. So I try skulking back to my cabin by devious corridors.

When they have finished dinner—around 7:45 p.m.—a major tidal upheaval occurs. First sitting ebbs from the dining room, migrating toward the show lounge for some preliminary dancing before their evening's entertainment fix. Before the next hungry tide floods into the dining room, every table must be cleared and reset, crumbs swept off chair seats; then it's second sitting's turn to dine. While they are at table, first sitting passengers' show runs its course and they ebb out of the show lounge, leaving it empty to await the flood of its second sitting audience.

Theoretically, once second sitting has, in turn, drained from the show lounge, the entire passenger load should well be flooding the public rooms. But many are still dispersed. Some are watching a movie, others gambling in the casino. Several dozen might be singing along with a singer-pianist or enjoying a quiz with one of the cruise staff. Bridge diehards and Scrabble players hold sway in the card room while a dedicated few will always be found gathered around the ship's jigsaw puzzle. Although some may merely be marking congenial time until the midnight buffet, a natural attrition has already set in as first-sitting passengers begin ebbing off to bed.

Jigsaw puzzles, incidentally, constitute an ideal shipboard pastime, a simple and unfailingly popular amusement by day or night that is open to all. Passengers clustered over a puzzle are achieving a task of mutual dedication, focus of repeated friendly encounters throughout the voyage. Once, aboard ROYAL PRINCESS, I saw the master, Captain Tony Yeomans, on one of his evening prowls about the public rooms, at work alone on the ship's puzzle, completely absorbed and preoccupied.

Given the cruise ship's carefully instigated demographic shifts, it should not be surprising that the two largest complementary spaces aboard every vessel must be the dining room and show lounge. Each must accommodate, with ease, half the passenger body. Once described simply as the main lounge, show lounges have evolved from a tables-and-chairs social venue into sophisticated maritime amphitheaters equipped with rows of theatrical seating. One of the nagging shortcomings aboard Holland-America's latest class of cruise ships is that the vessel's theater must serve (inadequately) as main lounge as well. However you slice it, the passenger body assembles in what remains an idle, theatrical auditorium.

It is there, every formal night, that the ship's singers, dancers and musicians mount substantial musical production shows. The scale and ambition of these colorful revues have escalated over the years. Rival cruise line impresarios are continually raising the entertainment ante, devising increasingly spectacular scenarios, more elaborate choreography, additional rhinestones and feathers, volumes of smoke, increasingly complex theatrical machinery and effects as well as the sound, at least, of ever larger orchestras and choruses. The musical and theatrical goal they seek is, for the most part, unrelenting Las Vegas—splashy, lavish and spectacular. But the score of every production show is eminently hummable, the sense of melodic *déjà vu* almost palpable. The shows' music directors play it very safe, adhering to hit-parade standards, targeted unerringly for the tastes of the cruise ship's placidly conservative, middle-brow, middle-aged, middle-American audience. In the business of shipboard amusement, uncontroversial familiarity is all.

In effect, a ship's show lounge never sleeps. Devoid of passengers, it serves during a portion of the day as rehearsal hall for brushing up production numbers or breaking in a cast replacement. During evenings between production shows, it plays host to perpetual entertainment of every kind. Cabaret is frequently the evening's bill of fare. The singers, specialty acts, magicians, jugglers and comics who tread the boards are figurative descendants of those thespian troupers who created vaudeville but perform today on the high seas instead. Rather than jump a passenger train

Furs, feathers and, always, a fortune in rhinestones: Show dancers Lori Burr and Diane Corlyon pose prettily aboard MONARCH OF THE SEAS. *Author's Collection*

to the next tank town, these airborne artistes jet around the globe for gigs aboard cruise ships. As opposed to the uncomplicated luggage logistics of the traveling harmonica virtuoso, consider the ticket counter ordeal of an itinerant magician who must wrestle hundreds of pounds of props, costumes, effects and caged doves or rabbits into aircraft holds en route to his ship.

At least once each cruise, the cruise staff mounts a special show that leans heavily and hilariously on enthusiastic passenger participation. I am always pleased at the retention of these amateur evenings because they keep alive an historic continuum from crossings past, aboard which self-generated fun was the order of the day. Throughout yesterday's ocean liners, home-brewed passenger amusement was the unvarying ritual; professional entertainers were never embarked. Similarly, today's passenger talent shows as well as masquerade evenings duplicate to perfection yesterday's shipboard regime. On non-Caribbean ships, there might well be a piano recital or perhaps some chamber music in the show lounge one evening.

In the late afternoon during some port calls, the show lounge may serve as venue for what is called *folklorico*, ethnic entertainment featuring troupes of amateur dance or choral societies booked temporarily from ashore. These presentations offer an unparalleled opportunity to sample some of the local culture, far more than can be absorbed fleetingly through tour bus windows.

Twice daily at sea, the show lounge turns into a giant bingo parlor. During the cruise, in addition to a ration of daily wins, a steadily accumulating jackpot game will attract bingo addicts to the cruise's final session, when a jackpot of several thousand dollars will be won by one ecstatic devotee at the conclusion of a final, cliff-hanging game. On one afternoon or evening, show lounge metamorphoses yet again into race-track for half a dozen, dice-driven horses, yet another time-honored shipboard staple from the old days.

The show lounge also sees use as a lecture hall, although that sort of cerebral passenger stimulation is more likely to be programmed on vessels plying worldwide itineraries rather than those idling about the Caribbean. Customary focus for daytime activities aboard Caribbean megaships is outdoors around the pool. Warm-weather indoor activities tend to be restricted to shore excursion talks, dance classes, lessons in napkin-folding or scarf tying, cooking demonstrations between meals in the dining room and, more recently, auctions of gaudily-framed artistic reproductions.

For large numbers of your fellow passengers, the ship's casino serves as irresistible lure by day and even more so at night. Once covers have been removed from blackjack tables, roulette wheels and crap table, the entire room bursts into frenetic life. During cruising's earliest days, shipboard gambling was usually franchised out. When the owners realized what vast revenues their casinos generated, they began operating them exclusively in-house.

In terms of on-board geography, the casino watchword is location, location and, yet again, location. You will never have trouble finding the casino aboard any vessel because the owners' invariable instruction to their naval architects is to site it blatantly along the most frequently traveled passenger thoroughfares. On some ships, you will find it impossible to enter the dining room without first passing through the casino; on others, you cannot achieve the vessel's atrium from your cabin without plodding inescapably through a hull-wide gambling den.

The designers employed to decorate casinos are torn between copying elegant and conservative gaming rooms in, let us say, London and Monte Carlo or reproducing, yet again, the conventional Nevadian prototype. Needless to say, as in shipboard show lounges, glitz seems to sell best so the thrust of casino décor is pure Las Vegas, designed to attract the lowest common denominators' eyes and ears alike. Walls and ceilings are lavishly studded with neon or chase lights while exotic decorative conceits occupy non-gaming niches. Completing the mood is a sometimes amplified, aural barrage of jangling, chirping, beeping electronic chatter, part of the overall intent to foment what is described in casino-speak as a compelling "buzz."

However shipboard designers strive to dress up their casino walls, it is really the rows of glistening slot machine facades that provide the dominant decorative motif, instant Las Vegas. However garish they may appear, it amuses me that the latest generation of slots boasts complex technology so advanced that it has reduced the chore of spinning those wheels to an effortless near-zero. Perched on well-upholstered stools, dedicated gamblers need never abandon their favored machine for a moment. Bills of every U.S. denomination can be fed into a convenient slot that instantly translates its value into machine credits, to be wagered electronically at will. Although the traditional right-hand pulling lever—the slot machine's equivalent of the Model T's engine crank—still functions if desired, the fast and effortless touch of a button is more often employed to set those maddening images in motion. (More plays per minute is the manufacturer's aim.) Small wins are registered instantly as electronic credits. The big jackpot's contagious racket is held in reserve for that electrifying moment when the traditional clattering metallic hemorrhage, buttressed by flashing lights and electronic chorus, broadcasts a spectacular win throughout the casino. Sustenance? Bar waiters circulate constantly. Relief? Designers of the latest vessels have included toilets within the casino for their patrons' convenience.

As an occasional roulette player, I sense that what enhances the appeal of table gaming is not only the prospect of winning but also of establishing a benign companionship with fellow players. Regulars, who gather nightly for sessions of roulette, blackjack or crap, become fast friends. I always remember Marie Anderson, who sailed with us aboard VEENDAM years ago; though prey to periodic, disastrous losing streaks, she confessed that she did not want to stop playing because she would then be deprived of what she referred to fondly as her "roulette buddies." Fellow gamblers

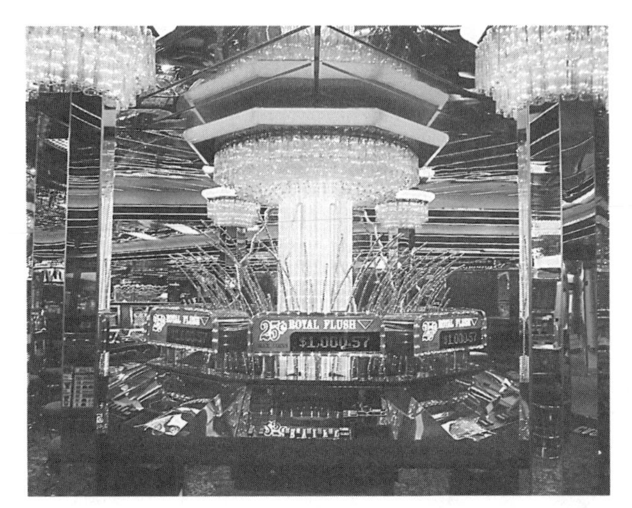

Neon, chrome, chase lights and noise enliven the casino aboard MAJESTY OF THE SEAS. On sister ship MONARCH OF THE SEAS, blackjack dealer Justin Tiesdell-Smith enjoys a moment's pause. *Barry M. Winiker*

persevering nightly against the odds relish their cozy, us-against-them camaraderie. The casino is, after all, one of the few public spaces, apart from tamer bingo or horse-racing, where lucky passengers can derive some serious revenue of their own.

Yet regardless, casino managers do their best to ensure that dealers and patrons remain strictly non-adversarial. An interdependent if cautious amiability is encouraged between casino staff and their clients. As part of their job, dealers must double as diplomats, dancing that delicate line separating hosting from hustling. Though the terms of their employment oblige them to maximize house revenue, they are always anxious at the same time to sustain an aura of bantering risk and fun with the customers. I remember one marvelously comic Lancashire dealer aboard ROYAL VIKING STAR nicknamed Tina. Whenever the roulette ball skittered to a stop on a non-wagered or "house" number, she would sweep away the multi-colored heap of losing chips, softening the blow, somehow, by proclaiming herself "Tina the Cleaner."

Theirs is demanding work. Dealing not only cards or chips, they must also deal tactfully and congenially with a segment of the passenger body whose financial reverses may sometimes be perceived as the dealer's doing. During their spells of table duty, they have to keep brisk track of an often bewildering array of bets, make change, handle cash-ins and pay-outs accurately under the eagle eyes of their superiors while at the same time keeping the table's money-making tempo up to speed. In addition to being deft of hand and eye, they must fulfill their social role as well, remaining agreeable and courteous, despite a repetitious barrage of the same hoary repartee they have heard for years. Frequent breaks away from the table are mandatory, customarily after a half-hour stint. Off-duty dealers curled up in a public room corner with a book and a coffee mug have earned that time off, essential respite from enervating, demanding, late-night toil.

As opposed to their shore-based confreres, shipboard gamblers are bona fide members of a shipboard community. Neither casual nor anonymous visitors to Las Vegas or Atlantic City, they have assumed residence on board, their cabins cheek by jowl with the casino. Given shipboard's intrinsic bonds, gambling passengers are, in effect, fellow souls with every crew member on board, ensuring an inevitable dealer/player symbiosis. Regardless how much cruise lines relish the earnings their casinos produce, they remain keenly aware that a perennially losing gambler, whether voluntarily player or no, may well become soured on the entire cruise experience if continuing losses are sustained within a company-endorsed facility.

I can still hear the agonized deliberation of one young honeymoon couple penetrating the wall from an adjacent cabin aboard COSTA RIVIERA. The wife was obviously near tears as, after several days' gambling losses in the casino, she and her new husband were totting up their remaining funds to ensure they could pay their tips and bar bills and make it home.

We cannot ring down the curtain on this nocturnal investigation without a few enthusiastic words about that popular evening passenger pastime, dancing. A selection of bands or combos play for dancing both before and after dinner all over the ship; later in the evening, a disc jockey will reign supreme in the discotheque. Passengers of every age remain enthusiastic dance aficionados, none more so, I have discovered, than veterans of World War II who still enjoy cutting a nostalgic rug with their wives. It should come as no surprise that the most popular standard played repeatedly aboard every vessel to this day is Glen Miller's *In the Mood.*

Passenger age or infirmity proves no barrier to the dance floor. I was astonished on a recent cruise to find how repeated evening dance sessions rejuvenated one tall octogenarian passenger. Limping slowly around the vessel by day, he always supported himself with a cane. But each night, the cane would be jettisoned as he sashayed eagerly and effortlessly onto the dance floor; the music as well as a succession of partners seemed to energize him for marathon, cane-free dancing.

On world cruises, which tend to book large numbers of widows, cruise lines recruit half a dozen of what are called social hosts, blazered, white-trousered and smooth-footed bachelors who remain on call in the various lounges and bars wherever music is playing. It is their job to make sure that any unattached lady who wishes to be waltzed around the floor will be accommodated.

Continued performance of vintage dance music has been ensured, curiously, by the collapse of the Berlin wall, the seminal event that put an end to Eastern European isolation. As a result, young musicians playing in many cruise ship orchestras are recruited increasingly from Russia, Poland or, indeed, from any number of formerly Soviet Union satellites. For example, on a recent NORWAY repositioning crossing, it turned out that every orchestral player on board was Russian. The musical strength of these eastern bloc players, frozen in time by the exigencies of the cold war, is perfectly attuned to the tastes of most passengers. American musicians, up-to-the-minute hip, look on these eastern interlopers with bemused indifference, dismissing them as hopelessly anachronistic, but the fact remains that most passengers like them.

A recent terpsichorean revelation is that there is always to be found on board most ships at least one impressive dancing couple from Japan. The vogue for western ballroom dancing all over the

Spread across the dance floor of NIEUW AMSTERDAM's Stuyvesant Lounge, passenger couples dance away the evening.
Barry M. Winiker

far east has spawned the occasional, talented Japanese cruising couple who have obviously dedicated hours of preparation and rehearsal to their dance-floor performance, far superior to the organized shuffle with which so many of their western fellow passengers—myself included—make do. Dance floors clear in admiration when these Japanese dance experts, always exquisitely dressed, can be persuaded onto the floor yet again.

I remember once staying at Venice's grandest hotel. On my way out of the dining room, I spotted a poster at the concierge's desk advertising a concert at the *Gran Teatro la Fenice*. Within three minutes, I was comfortably ensconced in a box awash with Mozart.

I tell the story with reason. One of Venice's many delights is that one can move about the city so expeditiously and conveniently. Liberated from the tyranny of the automobile, there is

A *thé dansant* aboard CRYSTAL HARMONY. Some passengers enjoy tea. *Barry M. Winiker*

neither traffic nor parking problem, merely the swift, impulsive amble of the footloose pedestrian.

Very much the same convenience characterizes your evenings aboard a cruise ship. Aspects of that same Venetian mystique are duplicated: You are surrounded by water, the night is filled with music, a heady ambience prevails and, most important, blessed proximity reigns supreme. The entire ship is at your disposal and somewhere throughout those congenial suites of public room, you will find diversions aplenty, more than one bound to amuse.

The cruise ship after dark encourages carefree and impulsive enjoyment. Why, you might even take some champagne out on deck and, like that cardboard couple that opened this chapter, commune with the moon.

CHAPTER VIII

Ashore and Back

I have been here before
But when or how I cannot tell;
I know the grass beyond the door,
The sweet keen smell,
The sighing sound, the lights around the shore.

—Dante Gabriel Rossetti

Knowst thou the land where the lemon trees bloom,
Where the gold orange glows in the deep thicket's gloom,
Where a wind ever soft from the blue heaven blows
And the groves are of laurel and myrtle and rose?

—Johann Wolfgang von Goethe

Why did they have to put the ruins so far from the ship?

—Complaint overheard on a bus returning from Mayan ruins at Chichén Iztá

Welcome to Lisbon, Portugal.

—Routine bridge announcement

Masters of cruise ships are often kind enough to invite me to join them on the bridge when we approach or leave a port. An extraordinary privilege, it is an invitation I always accept with equal parts alacrity and gratitude.

Arrivals entail very early mornings. I leave my cabin well before dawn, passing through deserted passenger corridors en route to the bridge, trying to time my arrival within the vessel's *sanctum sanctorum* prior to our rendezvous at the pilot station. I am buzzed through the pass door into that darkened world of hushed watchfulness, preoccupation, vigilance and brewing coffee. Conversation is terse and muted as shadowed silhouettes of captain, staff captain and officer of the watch hunch over glowing radar screens, monitoring the vessel's course and speed. It is purposely kept dark to improve night vision for the way ahead. The state of the engines' heartbeat is betrayed by dozens of pointillist telltale lights dotted atop sloping consoles. There is little noise save for an occasional warning buzz from an aggrieved electronic system that brings swift response and correction. From somewhere beyond our ken, heralded by a sustained cascade of atmospherics, a radioed voice disrupts the hush, conveying messages of anticipatory preparation from shore.

Within a curtained alcove away from the wheel, the navigation officer works intently beneath a shaded lamp, poring over the chart and updating the vessel's progress. Wielding parallel rules, dividers and sharpened pencil, he repeatedly diagrams the course of our cautious approach.

Beyond the bridge windows, his virtual plot as well as the elongated green images from the radar screens come to actual life as, in the half-light before dawn, a suspicion of land mass materializes. Early-bird passengers with binoculars and cameras at the ready are clustered along a crescent of lookout deck immediately below the bridge, peering into the gloom. Their vigil is rewarded as daylight starts to erode the night sky. On the bridge, there comes that intriguing moment when random constellations of twinkling lights adorning land ahead mimic to perfection the glowing electronic pinpoints clustered atop bridge consoles. That momentary, privately observed juxtaposition always delights me.

Gull outriders soar effortlessly alongside, riding our hull thermals. We slow to accommodate the pilot boat, a bustling emissary from shore speeding for our flank that leaves a crescent of wake across the limpid harbor approaches. Subsequent entry of the pilot himself into the wheel house breaks the spell. He greets the master with a newspaper and accepts a cup of coffee from the bridge boy in return. After examining the waters ahead, he reconfirms our course and orders a resumption of speed. The pilot from shore, who knows these harbor waters well, has temporarily "taken the con," assumed control of the vessel, albeit with the sometimes reluctant blessing of the master.

Bridges aboard most of today's cruise ships are closed, their entire length encased in plate glass to protect expensive navigational instruments against ubiquitous salt damp. If he wants to look down at the dock, the master does so through a glass panel set into the deck at his feet. Encapsulated within those sealed aeries, captains are unable to feel a crosswind on their cheeks; wind speed and direction must be read instead on a dial convenient to every maneuvering station. Oilskins are no longer required on the bridge for all ship handling is achieved under cover; caps are no longer worn for arrival. Cocooned in their glass aeries, masters are also denied any conversational exchanges—which most of them seem genuinely to enjoy—with the respectful passenger gallery that always gathers above open bridge wings to observe the delicate process of maneuvering that will bring the vessel to its anchorage or alongside a dock. Closed bridges isolate their occupants from everyone else on board.

The rising sun's flat, golden light throws details of the land into sharp relief. This is the same revelatory light that illuminates the Statue of Liberty for vessels entering the port of New York, the Corcovado overlooking Guanabara Bay for arrival in Rio de Janeiro, or the marble and brick spire of Venice's Campanile that towers over the city. By that early daylight, dense electric clusters ahead are revealed as rival cruise ships already tied up alongside or approaching placidly in our wake. We can spy dozens of tour busses already drawn up on the pier, ready to drive disembarking passengers to overland adventures. As our approach continues, the sounds, sights and smells of shore envelop the open decks. I always relish entry into the Bermudian port of St. George's, as the vessel snakes through worrisomely narrow Town Cut to achieve harbor. Though that tight entrance may give master and pilot pause, it is an approach that delights every passenger because, suddenly, magically, the fragrance of bougainvillea is wafted seductively across the waters, incomparable sensory contact with that enchanted isle.

Once we are within reach of the pier, from mooring decks forward and aft, messenger lines are flung ashore to waiting stevedores who use them to haul the ship's hawsers across the shrinking gap separating hull from dock. Spring lines are secured first, stout ties that prevent the vessel's forward or after movement. Once they have been slacked off or tautened to suit the gangway's location, long forward and aft moorings are secured next, fixing the vessel's pier position irrevocably. Last of all, breast lines, hawsers that secure the vessel directly adjacent to the dock, are snugged tight once bow- and stern-thrusters have moved the vessel improbably sideways. (Thrusters are propellers in transverse tunnels at bow or stern that pierce the hull from port to starboard; these are invaluable maneuvering weapons in every cruise ship's mooring arsenal, almost completely obviating the need for harbor tugs.) Only after the breast

Cautiously, NORWEGIAN SKY negotiates the narrow channel into St George's. An anticipatory scenting of Bermudian flowers permeates the open decks. *Barry M. Winiker*

lines have been made fast will the master, from his commanding perch overlooking the pier, return the rudder amidships and signal to the chief below that he is finished with engines.

Immobilized alongside at last, the ship stilled and mute, the on-board focus shifts abruptly from over the bow to over the side. Passengers who have been transfixed by the process of docking leave vantage points at the railing and repair below for breakfast. Then comes the task of girding themselves for shore.

Once the gangway has been rigged, first across it is a ship-bound flock of immigration and customs officials whom the purser welcomes on board with a buffet of orange juice, coffee and rolls within the temporarily off-limits seclusion of the card room. Following their deliberations, the ship is cleared and passengers—some of them extremely anxious—are finally free to go ashore. The ship will remain in port throughout the day, from approximately eight in the morning until six at night.

If the port is a new one where cruise ships rarely call, you will bear witness to a unique, two-way confrontation of land/sea wonderment. In citing this phenomenon, I am indebted to my dear Norwegian friend and colleague, Bård Kolltveit, who first suggested it to me years ago. Picture a vessel gliding in to anchor for the first time off a primitive coast. To awestruck locals, the dawn apparition of that white, late-twentieth century marvel seems like a wondrous spaceship that has miraculously touched down from another world.

That sense of disbelief works both ways. The occupants of the spaceship, gazing down at the shore from the fastness of their ultramodern conveyance, are confronted by an equally alien spectacle. To them, the primitive hordes and huts crowding the shoreline seem just as astonishing, as though Martians have materialized from another planet. So there exists, between ship and shore, a doubled, reflective incredulity, encountered at the chance interface of two contrasting cultures, each equally amazed and astonished at the other's existence.

Every stop along a cruise's itinerary is either a tendering port—requiring the use of the ship's motorized tenders to achieve land from an offshore anchorage—or a docking port, permitting swift, easy disembarkation directly onto the pier. The difference between merely tripping down the gangway as opposed to transferring into a small boat secured alongside an anchored ship is largely one of convenience. Passengers aboard a docked ship can come and go as they please, making several visits into town, if desired, interspersed with restorative interludes on board. But tendering passengers, facing cumulative delays of awaiting the arrival of a tender, riding it to shore and disembarking at the pier, will probably restrict their outings to one. Then too, if seas are rough, disembarkation down a companionway or through the hull into a tender, particularly for the elderly, may be challenging. If sea conditions are really bad, the captain of an anchored vessel may haul his tenders back up into their davits and write off the port completely. At risk is not only the difficulty of getting his passengers safely ashore but also, if the weather deteriorates, retrieving them. No master wants to have any of his precious human cargo stranded ashore, putting the balance of his itinerary at risk.

Regardless, I cherish a soft spot for the ritual of going ashore by tender, partly because it has always been the traditional means of achieving a tropical port and partly because it keeps your vessel at a distance, detached from sometimes unappealing waterfronts. Anchored peacefully offshore and enjoying a cool sea breeze beats baking alongside a humid pier.

It would be safe to say that the vast majority of passengers going ashore will have booked themselves onto one of several choices of shore excursions. Every cruise ship has what is called a "shorex" (shore excursion) office, staffed by an efficient team of company employees. Either their chief, the shorex manager, or, if there is one, a regular port lecturer presents illustrated talks in the lounge several days before arrival in every port, documenting the length, nature and cost of excursions available to passengers. Televised, preview snippets of the same excursions are shown repeatedly on cabin television as well.

Some excursions may have already taken place even before the cruise begins. Cruise lines offer their clientele what are called pre-

and post-cruise packages that bracket the beginning and end of every voyage. By taking advantage of these optional offerings, passengers can arrange for a night or two ashore in a hotel from which additional tours have been organized to investigate and explore the port and its environs more fully. Those pre-cruise packages are invaluable for the jet-lagged, offering some restful downtime to recuperate from the ravages of flight prior to the day of embarkation. And for distant ports rich with cultural offerings, it is a marvelous way of maximizing what may well be your only visit to that part of the world.

Shore excursions for sale on board in connection with each successive port will vary in duration, their length dependent on travel time between the pier and various destinations. Some can consume an entire day, incorporating a necessary stop for lunch along the way. For example, when a cruise ship ties up at Port Said, there follows a three-hour bus ride across the desert to Cairo. Once arrived in the capital, the scheduling is tight but necessarily so. There must be time for entry into the National Museum, lunch at a hotel, a visit to the pyramids, a glimpse of the sphinx and even a short if inevitably tempestuous camel ride before re-boarding the bus for the long trek back to the ship. That is a classic all-day tour, similar in duration and requiring the same passenger stamina as inspecting jungle-clad Mayan ruins in Mexico's hinterland or being driven up into the mountainous interior of Costa Rica's capital of San José from Puerto Caldera on the country's steamy Pacific coast.

Typical half-day tours might include bussing from the pier at Naples to Pompeii's fascinating remains an hour south of the port, or visiting Winchester Cathedral while docked at Southampton. There might well be even shorter tours, a two-hour drive around a downtown area to get a flavor of the city or a visit to a nearby cultural landmark. For popular destinations, these shorter excursions are customarily scheduled for either morning or afternoon or both, with a convenient gap in between for lunch in the vessel's dining room.

In fact, returning to eat their midday meal on board is an option of which almost all cruise passengers avail themselves. Admittedly, it makes economic sense because that on-board meal has already been paid for as part of the cruise's ticket price. Then too, some passengers are uneasy about ordering unfamiliar dishes in a strange tongue at an alien restaurant, fearful of either food poisoning, ridicule, gouging or all three.

I wish they might be persuaded otherwise. One of my primary reasons for going ashore is in quest of an adventurous lunch. In Japanese ports, it is supposedly ruinously expensive to eat in any restaurant. In my experience, those are places that cater expensively to tourists, offering Kobe beef, imported wines and western pretension. Mary and I always prefer the inexpensive pleasure of ducking through the low doorway of almost any noodle shop for a bowl of that inexpensive, incomparable *ramen* or, even easier, investigating the wide selection of modestly priced meals available in every large department store.

One of my favorite shoreside lunches was in the Turkish port of Kusadasi where we found an extremely simple but good restaurant along the waterfront, its terrace shaded from the sun. Giant GRAND PRINCESS loomed placidly nearby. And who can resist, when calling at Funchal, lunch up on the vine-covered terrace of Reed's Hotel, with the harbor's panorama spread invitingly below?

The great advantage of organized shore excursions is that they are, in a sense, completely effortless for the passenger. Everything is prearranged—transportation, meals if appropriate, an English-speaking guide, immunity from beggars or touts, tickets of entry into park or ruins and, perhaps most important of all for anxious shore excursionists, the guarantee that the ship will not sail until every busload has been logged safely back on board. By contrast, if you travel independently, you should keep firm track of the time to make sure that you re-embark well before sailing; if independent travelers are late or delayed, the vessel will have no compunction about sailing without them.

There are exceptions to the bleak finality of this eventuality but they are rare. I was once on a vessel tied up in Le Havre and a couple who had taken a train up to Paris that morning telephoned the ship to report that they had missed their return train and were racing north by taxi. The Parisian driver, unfamiliar with rural Norman geography, got hopelessly lost and by the time he and the embarrassed couple drew up at the pier, the passenger body applauded derisively while the master and his officers glowered unhappily from the bridge wing. Then again, during the same day that Mary and I were lunching along Kusadasi's waterfront, Billy Vader, one of the ship's entertainers, was racing to get back to the ship by taxi following a hectic independent excursion far inland. Coming over the crest of a hill, though vastly relieved to spot his vessel, he was then dismayed to realize that because GRAND PRINCESS is so vast, she appeared closer than she really was. But he did manage to make it back to the pier at the last moment before departure.

On the subject of company-organized versus independent shore excursions, I must confess to mixed emotions. Although one can absorb a certain amount through the combination of a bus window and an intelligible guide, I dislike the sense of sanitized insulation from the sights, sounds and smells of the city or countryside. Encased within their secure but sometimes claustrophobic conveyance, embussed visitors to foreign parts are too often deprived of the full sensory experience of abroad. Admittedly, for the elderly or infirm, the tour bus is a godsend. Nevertheless, its occupants are perennially short-changed, over-protected perhaps from jarring realities but denied the opportunity of savoring the full sensory spectrum.

I remember so well a call at Vladivostok aboard SKY PRINCESS during one of her seasonal repositioning crossings from Alaska to the Far East. Mary and I set off on our own, walking easily around that neglected city, passing through crowds of Russian pedestrians en route. Several times, teen-age schoolgirls stopped us, begging charmingly for our names and addresses to record in their exercise books, desperate for any possible liaison with Americans. Their unhappiness with their municipal infrastructure was understandable. Save for its over-restored transcontinental railway station, little of interest enlivens this neglected Far Eastern outpost. Most buildings are drab, paint is faded and peeling, streets are catastrophically potholed and, years of *glasnost* notwithstanding, the shops remain virtually empty.

Throughout the morning, we kept running into dozens of our fellow passengers embarked on the port's sole shore excursion. Their tour busses lumbered awkwardly through the same streets along which we strolled. Instead of clambering in and out of the bus, as well as waiting for the inevitable latecomers, they could just as easily, less expensively and far more evocatively, have achieved the same objectives on foot by themselves.

Of course, many passengers sensibly combine the two touring modes, embarking on a tour bus for a distant destination in the morning and spending their afternoon rambling through the port on foot. Appropriate behavior for passengers traveling ashore in a foreign land by themselves involves little more than common sense: Dress sensibly and conservatively, wear comfortable shoes and try not standing vulnerably on street corners consulting a large map. You may be propositioned by any number of guides or touts, anxious to conduct you on a visit to a local attraction. In the event you decide to take them up on their offer, make sure that you thoroughly understand what the final cost will be. Similarly, if you decide to board a local taxi, establish without fail the tariff for your prospective journey with the driver before setting off; this will avoid the possibility of an unpleasant standoff once you reach your destination and are stiffed with an exorbitant price.

Ports of call represent for nearly all passengers an ideal opportunity to shop and it is a rare bus tour that does not incorporate somewhere within its peregrination a stop at a souvenir outlet or market. I often wonder: Does sea air encourage passenger acquisitiveness or is it merely that contemporary Americans, unable to renounce their predilection for hometown malls, are determined to perpetuate buying sprees abroad?

Whatever the reason, Americans seem unable to resist the temptation of a bargain wherever it may lie. Gratifying "shopportunities" abound from port to port, none more appealing than the legendary West Indian island of St. Thomas, inescapable crossroads of every Caribbean itinerary. It is a rare day when less than half a dozen cruise ships, some of them the world's largest, cannot be found tied up in or anchored off the port, disgorging armies of passengers intent on what the British describe inventively as "retail therapy."

Large areas of Caribbean ports serve as tropical malls and, save for street vendors or pier hustlers, the time-honored marketplace ritual of bargaining has been subsumed by the efficient burble of the electronic cash register. Only in the Middle and Far East or most African ports can passengers still be indulged with traditional sessions of bargaining; indeed, it is part of every local merchant's marketing strategy.

I must confess that haggling is not my strong suit; I dislike the tiresome cut and thrust of bargaining. Not for me the protracted rit-

Going ashore by tender, ROYAL VIKING SEA passengers disembark in Norway's Geiranger Fjord. *Author's Collection*

ual the aficionado bargainer relishes—the feigned indifference, the repeated low-ball offer, the turn-your-back-and-walk-away ploy, followed by a cautious return for yet another bout of contentious bidding. Although my cousin Claudia delights in opening negotiations by offering shopkeepers exactly half of what they initially demand, I prefer to avoid the entire procedure.

Sometimes, blessedly, merely the passage of time works wonders, obviating any need for haggling. I once disembarked onto the pier in Colombo to explore the makeshift market that local merchants had set up in the shade of ROTTERDAM's great blue bow. Among the tourist gimcracks on the counter of one stall, I spied a miniature carved ivory elephant, rigged with the glittery, bejeweled caparison of temple pachyderms from inland Kandy. Since the stall holder's price was far higher than I thought it should be, I walked on.

But returning back on board near sailing time, I discovered that prices throughout that pier-side market had dropped precipitously in anticipation of ROTTERDAM's imminent departure for Bombay. As a result, out at sea that evening, the little Sri Lankan elephant stood triumphantly on the ledge of my porthole. Yet, however remarkable the reduction in price, I am quite convinced that the wily Sinhalese dealer who sold it to me had doubtless realized a handsome profit, the same one he had anticipated when setting up shop that morning.

For many, the lure of the chase is overwhelming and passenger bargains, particularly on world cruises, accumulate at an alarming rate. Cloisonné, rattan, brassware and lacquer start to crowd every cabin. But the downside of that bountiful harvest is getting it home: How will that Turkish carpet, the Benares brass tray, those Chinese vases, the teak end table or the Balinese carvings survive the plane ride at cruise's end? Small wonder that one of the most well-attended events the day before disembarkation is a white elephant sale in the main lounge, during which quantities of donated, ill-advised exotica can be snapped up for a song. Nevertheless, one intriguing question remains: How is it that cumbersome items apparently too awkward to fly as part of passenger A's luggage are somehow happily transported home by passenger B? Whatever the outcome of the white elephant sale, I am pleased to report that my personal white elephant—the little ivory miniature from Sri Lanka—fitted easily into my briefcase.

One of my favorite and most heartfelt shipboard sights of all time was a sign that used to hang above the gangways of all Royal Viking

MARDI GRAS and SKYWARD bracket a nighttime pier in the Mexican port of Cozumel. Within an hour, both vessels will slip away into the sub-tropical night. *Barry M. Winiker*

tonnage. Daubed across the rubber cushion protecting tall passenger heads from the port door's unforgiving steel margins were two immensely reassuring words: WELCOME HOME. After an exhausting day of overland excursion, however rewarding, exchanging the hugger-mugger of ashore for the serenity of aboard remains one of cruising's recurring delights.

Whereas the vessel's arrival in port, whether anchored out or tied up, is of necessity a cautious procedure, departure that same evening seems in comparison almost lighthearted. As daylight wanes, tour busses unload their frazzled occupants and the last shopping fanatics tear themselves away from just one more bargain among the pierside stalls. Throughout the vessel's final half-hour in port, over the loudspeaker system, the officer of the watch has repeatedly intoned his solemn warning, urging all who are not sailing with the ship to disembark. Longshoremen gather laconically at each bollard, waiting on command from the ship to shrug off the same hawsers that they had so laboriously capped that morning.

The pilot embarks and mounts once more to the bridge, ready to help navigate the vessel out of port. There, he will find the staff captain in radio communication with subordinate officers, one posted at the bow, another at the stern, as well as the security officer manning the gangway amidships. During the remaining moments before sailing, multiple hawsered ties to shore are reduced, from three to two to final achievement of that tether of imminent departure which seamen describe as "singled up," with only one line securing bow or stern. Then, by radioed command from the staff captain, the gangway is dismantled and brought on board, its port door through the shell plating sealed.

At the appointed hour, the vessel is, as it is prosaically described, undocked. Once singled lines are slipped, bow- and stern-thrusters surge, creating underwater turmoil alongside the pier, churning up bottom mud as the vessel renounces all shore ties and moves implacably away from her day-long mooring.

At St. Thomas, surfeited as it is with hundreds of sailings annually, the departure of yet another cruise ship arouses scant interest or attention. But in Canada's maritime provinces, for example, or in remote Norwegian coastal towns unaccustomed to regular cruise ship visits, the port's inhabitants turn out to wave the vessel off. There are always lots of children in attendance and, if I have remembered to buy a bag, I often fling wrapped candy down to them.

I lament the sad diminution of sailings enriched with paper serpentines, those streamers that contribute to such festive departures but also, alas, to litter and, it is said, pollution. Regardless, the Japanese especially cling to that fond ritual of maritime farewell and I remember quite clearly one emotional leave taking from Hakodate. Distributed on board were serpentines of some stronger stuff

Bon Voyage, yesterday and today: (above) Almost totally obscured by serpentines, RMS ORMONDE is about to depart from Honolulu in the 1920's. (left) In an age of ecological awareness, as NORDIC PRINCE sails, passengers and a more modest display of serpentines adorn the railing. *Author's Collection and Barry M. Winiker*

than paper, a kind of reinforced plastic that parted with difficulty. From among the forest of multi-colored links lacing ship to shore, one vibrant pink strand survived. Holding the pier end was a ravishingly attractive young woman. It was not immediately clear to those of us hanging over the promenade deck who was clutching the corresponding shipboard end. Maybe it was a dear friend about to sail or, more likely, no one special, merely a passenger who had lucked out. As the vessel undocked and moved away from land, one by one, every existing connective thread was sundered until only the one held by the girl sustained that fragile ship-to-shore connection. Hoping to extend that connection to the very end, she darted down the pier, following the ship to maintain her tenuous link. The entire passenger gallery observed and applauded her feat. But, of course, that last pink strand was inevitably parted by the vessel's movement and a great moan went up. Heartened, the girl waved and blew kisses as our ship stood out to sea. We all waved back.

Beyond the harbor, out by the pilot station at the end of the channel, the morning's logistics are reversed. The pilot bids farewell and is escorted by a junior officer down a specially reserved elevator to the open shell door where the pilot boat awaits. He clambers down the Jacob's ladder and, before vanishing below, waves up to the staff captain on the bridge wing. "Pilot's off," the latter imparts laconically and the ship's hull is sealed against the moment of another pilot's arrival in the next port.

As the pilot boat turns and speeds for shore, the convention of maritime leave-taking mandates a whistled exchange between two parting (or indeed, any passing) vessels. Three long, measured blasts, first from the pilot boat, then three in booming response from the larger ship. But that is not all: Tradition demands another, final toot—a brief peck on the cheek, as it were—to complete the ritual. That additional, final exchange is based, I am convinced, on the ancient nautical admonition so accurately sung by the sailor chorus in Gilbert & Sullivan's *HMS Pinafore*: "Give three cheers and one cheer more." With that one cheer more delivered, the two vessels draw apart.

Free of the port, the ship reverts to her native element. Out on both mooring decks, once carefully coiled hawsers have been re-shrouded beneath protective tarpaulins, seamen with pots of white paint apply a protective coat to the fairlead flanges or rollers where, throughout the day, hawsers have silently chafed those curving planes down to bare steel. Those essential mooring surfaces are the most often re-painted portions of the vessel, scarred by hundreds of docking and undockings.

I am continually struck by one singular and unfailing legacy of a port day. Paradoxically, temporary fragmentation of our floating community has somehow strengthened and enriched shipboard bonds. Like crusaders returning home triumphantly from an arduous campaign in foreign climes, passengers re-embarking after a day in the hinterlands enjoy nothing more than sharing every detail of their adventure. As a result, the level of conversation in the dining room on the evening of a port day, particularly the first one, is measurably more intense than ever before, the decibel count ratcheting up as passengers regale each other with their war stories.

CHAPTER IX

THE CREW, GOD BLESS 'EM

"J" for jolly Jack tar, come ashore for the day
To enjoy a good lark and get rid of his pay,
With his "Shiver my timbers!" "Avast" and "Belay"
And other strange things which these naval men say.

—-Captain Seecombe, *Army & Navy Drolleries*, 1885

Sigh no more, ladies, sigh no more,
Men were deceivers ever,
One foot in sea, and one on shore,
To one thing constant never . . .

—William Shakespeare, *Much Ado About Nothing*

Life in a closed community such as a ship can impose pressures which are not present in shore environments.

—Cautionary written advice imparted to newly embarking crew

Does the crew all live on board?

—Query from a SAGAFJORD passenger
addressed to a casino dealer, 1982

It seems unfortunate that the first encounter between passengers and crew must take place the day you board your ship; just as unfortunately, there is no way to avoid it. For the day of your embarkation is also the day of the previous passenger-load's disembarkation. Cruise lines call it turnaround day, an alpha-and-omega interface between two consecutive voyages when thousands check out of the floating hotel in the morning and thousands more check in that same afternoon.

For the crew, turnaround day demands patience, forbearance and, for many, backbreaking labor. Old passengers, familiar with the vessel and its routine, are leaving, to be replaced by confused newcomers who will require preliminary handholding and directions as they mill about corridors and companionways. The "You Are Here" ship's cutaway elevations and deck plans get a strenuous workout on turnaround day.

Small wonder that by the time the ship sails, most of those working on board are stressed out. By the same token, hallmark of a well-trained, resilient crew and sound shipboard management is that, regardless of the logistical challenges the crew has just endured, embarking passengers are welcomed as they should be.

The ordeal really begins the night previous, when suitcases appear in the corridors, locked and labeled for shore as passengers deposit them outside their cabin doors for pickup. Every ship has a corps of cleaners, men and women whose mopping, vacuuming, dusting and polishing starts at midnight and who customarily retire to bed as passengers first stir. It is from that nocturnal force that personnel are dragooned as the ship's baggage handlers. From sunset of that penultimate cruising day, they roam passenger country with trolleys until well past midnight, gathering up a staggering accumulation of luggage that must be manhandled, within temporarily padded elevators, to a lower deck area against the moment of off-loading on the morrow. Their task is made no easier by the certain knowledge that within 24 hours, they will repeat the procedure in reverse, distributing the new passenger-load's incoming luggage to every cabin.

If you've ever a mind for it, take the trouble to visit that lower luggage deck some time late on your last night, to appreciate, first-hand, the luggage team's backbreaking achievement. You will find an Everest—nay, a Himalayan range—of suitcases towering to the ceiling. Nearly all will be black, color of choice for many of today's travelers. Some try distinguishing their black suitcase from other black suitcases by attaching a red yarn pompom to its handle. But it is a curious fact that America's pompom color of choice is also red; as a result, that imposing black luggage facade is festooned like Rockefeller Center's Christmas tree with dozens of matching red pompoms.

The purser's staff is up at the crack of dawn on turnaround day for they have spent many hours of the previous 24 updating passengers' shipboard account. Before any charges can be transferred irrevocably to pre-signed credit card imprints, preliminary copies of the final reckoning are slipped beneath cabin doors for verification.

How sobering those printouts, your cruise indulgence in review; be grateful that meal consumption has not been documented so remorselessly. Arrayed in dense columns is a cumulative torrent of drinks—from poolside cocktail to dining room vintage, from after-dinner cappuccino to late-night beer, from bottled water shorex ration to eye-opening bloody Mary. Shopping debits appear as well, logo clothing, perfume or jewelry extravagances one after the other. Lurking elsewhere among those relentless columns you will find every photograph, gangway candid or formal portrait, every telephone call, fax or e-mail, every shore excursion and shuttle bus charge, every spa indulgence or laundry and dry cleaning charge and most shattering of all, perhaps a horrendous cash advance signed impulsively late at night at the cashier's cage in the casino.

Initial reaction to that startling financial cold shower is incredulity: Did we really wallow in all that drink? Were all those gewgaws from the shops really necessary? Some try disputing the official record so assistant pursers must steel themselves near turnaround day to deal with the aggrieved intent on verification. But the evidence is irrefutable. Although every passenger is encouraged to retain the originals of their signed charge slips, only the hyper-methodical bother. But what passengers may have ignored or misplaced, the ship's eagle-eyed accountants have not. Sheaves of buttressing carbons can be dredged up for passenger review, some still adorned with forensic stigmata—a suntan-oiled thumbprint on a pool drink charge or motes of peanut dust adhering to another from the bars. Predictably, chagrined clientele primed for battle turn away from the purser's desk, if not mollified at least resigned to the scale of their shipboard appetites.

As do their assistant purser shipmates, the patient army of cabin stewards prepares for the impact of mass defection. The song of the vacuum cleaner is heard throughout the vessel. In reluctantly vacated cabins, wastebaskets overflow with an accumulation of cruising redundancies: withered flowers, empty bottles, discarded wrappings, bruised fruit and the inevitable detritus of shipboard ephemera—cocktail party invitations, daily programs, fellow passengers' business cards and, yes, perhaps even a thwarted collection of charge slip originals.

Since every bed must be stripped and made up fresh, handrails along cabin corridors are festooned with fresh folded linen. Throughout the voyage, linen changes were staggered cabin by cabin; but on this day of days, every berth must be made up anew.

Carts laden with dirty sheets, towels and terry cloth bathrobes are wheeled along to the nearest crew elevator en route down to the laundry. The turmoil of turnaround day is particularly hard on the ship's laundry staff because gargantuan loads must be run through the washers, then dried, ironed, folded and returned to the fray. One small way, incidentally, that every passenger can lessen laundry men's burden aboard ship is *never* to fold their napkins at meal's end. Every one that is must be unfolded again before it enters the washer.

One of the strangest disembarkations I have ever experienced marked completion of venerable ROTTERDAM's final cruise of 1998, after nearly 40 years' service. On that historic occasion, cabin corridors were unnaturally serene. Once linen had been stripped from the beds, none replaced it, nor were vacuum cleaners called into play. No embarking passengers were expected for weeks because later that day, ROTTERDAM would sail north from Fort Lauderdale to Newport News, to undergo interior transformation into REMBRANDT. The spectacle of those empty, abandoned cabins, no less than the uncommon silence, was surreal.

Not so aboard vessels expecting a new influx of clients later that day. By noon, every cabin along every deck must be laboriously restored to brochure perfection, complete with welcome aboard program, filled ice bucket, sample bottle of water, fruit, and, for VIPs, a bottle of chilled champagne and two glasses. The time pressure is intense as chief steward's assistants on the prowl tally the roster of completed cabins. Dining room stewards experience their own special purgatory early on the morning of turnaround day. Passengers, dispossessed of their cabins and burdened with hand luggage, surge in distractedly for their final meal. Last breakfasts are notorious gastronomic fixtures, conventionally dished up for murderers awaiting execution. Quipped "condemned" Bob Hope's character in the opening scene of one 1950s film, "This is the *worst* last breakfast I've ever had!"

Resonances of the comedian's gallows humor permeate cruise ship dining rooms on turnaround day, not only among passengers morose that their cruise is over but even more so, among stewards whose job it is to serve them. Maîtres d'hôtel, sous chefs, captains and stewards are unanimous in reporting that last breakfasts in ships' dining rooms are hell. As though determined to drain the final measure of their cruise's cup, passengers routinely over-order—eggs of every description, bacon and sausage to excess, waffles, pancakes, toast and Danish pastries galore. Stewards are kept on the perpetual hop, running back and forth to the pantry for unreasonable and frequently uneaten meals.

For disaffected passengers, especially those who have partied sentimentally into the wee hours, the gloom of that last breakfast is further sullied by hangover. Similarly, it is their stewards' morning after as well, the morning after disbursement of tips. The bills folded within those sometimes furtively proffered envelopes the night previous will raise—or lower—every recipient's financial morale for the week to come.

Since tips serve as a veritable barometer of shipboard contentment, they should command our most scrupulous attention. Herewith an attempt, if not of a complete exposé, at least some valuable insight into the conundrum of shipboard tipping. I shall touch on not only its history but also the status—or non-status—of the practice throughout today's cruise industry. And since this chapter is ostensibly devoted to the crew, surely there is no more sensitively crew-related topic.

Aboard history's first ocean liners, whether powered by sail, steam or both, passengers were expected to tip dining saloon and cabin personnel. While most did, either generously or grudgingly, some inevitably refused. Perhaps not surprisingly, Americans, bountiful spenders and internationally susceptible soft touches in so many respects, were always shipboard's most generous tippers, distributing largesse on an often heroic scale. Stewards aboard both QUEEN ELIZABETH and QUEEN ELIZABETH 2, for example, confide that they far prefer waiting on Americans as opposed to their fellow countrymen. Certain Englishmen abroad, still imbued with outmoded Raj expectations, boast insufferable shipboard manners.

A horrendous case in point: Scarcely did one pink-faced Briton sit down to dine on the first night of his Royal Caribbean cruise that he informed the steward loudly that he could not "possibly enjoy my dinner because this tablecloth is improperly starched." The maître d'hôtel was summoned and the cloth changed, to the disbelief and inconvenience of his tablemates. But that was only the Brit's opening salvo. The next night, his baked potato was the villain: "You don't honestly expect me to eat a potato with an eye in it, do you?" A presumably eyeless baked potato was rushed from the galley. On the third night, the tarnished underside of a serving platter prompted yet another outburst.

Presumably, this dreadful little man imparted a complaint *du jour* for the entire cruise but we shall never know, because my informant—another Britisher—and his wife jumped table. The maître d'hôtel said first that a change was impossible; but on discovering that the passengers were refugees "from table 25," space was immediately found across the room. I wonder if that Britisher left any tips; my guess is that he did not. The British do not necessarily monopolize outrageous shipboard behavior; bad apples of every nationality fester within every dining room barrel.

Quite naturally, shipping companies are loath to discourage the practice of tipping because it underwrites the bulk of their stewards' salaries. The base pay for stewards today—many but not all of them from the third world—seldom exceeds $300 a month. However, a hard-working bedroom or dining room steward looking after a dozen clients can supplement that total by several hundred additional dollars at the end of every cruise. For stewards from the Philippines or Indonesia, income of that kind transforms them into relatively rich men and women. Hence, the brimming worldwide pool of applicants clamoring for shipboard jobs.

More recently, since the collapse of the iron curtain, Rumanians, Yugoslavs, Hungarians, Poles and Czechs have entered the market as well, in quest of an anticipated dollar return unthinkable within their local economies. And those who dispense most of those rewards are inevitably you, generous Americans who make up more than 80% of cruise ship passenger loads around the globe.

Though tips are almost always disbursed at cruise's end, there are exceptions. World cruise passengers, for example, are encouraged to tip stewards periodically throughout their circumnavigation. Additionally, there are some passengers who prefer paving their shipboard way with tips immediately upon embarkation, the unspoken implication being that the generosity of that first installment will be duplicated at cruise's end.

But most give out tips on the last night of the voyage. Indeed, near cruise's end, passengers all over the vessel become preoccupied with the task. They pick up special envelopes set out near the purser's desk and there is a run on twenties, tens and fives.

Before leaving your cabin on your last night, leave an envelope for your steward prominently on pillow or bureau so that he or she finds it when turning down your bed; the remainder go with you to the dining room. In fact, all passengers descending for their final dinner have pockets stuffed with envelopes; later that evening, dining room personnel will descend in turn to their quarters, pockets stuffed with the same envelopes.

Incidentally, apart from passenger bingo, horse race or casino winnings, that unrestricted greenback traffic represents the fourth and only additional cash flow permitted aboard ship; all other transactions are routed scrupulously through the vessel's electronic charge system.

Distributing tips is easy; more demanding is the debate about how much should be inserted into each envelope. Though all companies circulate tipping guide lines for their clients, I propose adding my two cents' worth as well. I do so reluctantly, only because it is risky to quote figures that will continue to make realistic sense for the life of this volume. Nevertheless, the attempt must be made for it is precisely this kind of hard information that Nonpax crave. By way of economic reference, the figures that follow date from 1999; be aware that inflation may well take its toll as we lurch into our third millennium.

Stewards should be tipped a minimum of $3 per day *per passenger*. Adhering to this formula, a couple's basic tips for a week at sea add up to $42 for your cabin steward, another $42 for your dining room waiter and slightly less—perhaps $30—for the less experienced busboy. Basic, almost inescapable total thus far is $114. Of course, these are acceptable minimums. Obviously, if you are pleased with a particular steward's performance, he or she will certainly not object if you exceed the amounts suggested above.

Note above that I purposefully use the phrase "dining room personnel" because you have the option of rewarding peripheral staff in the dining room in addition to your steward. In fact, dining room captain and maître d'hôtel alike try their level best *not* to be peripheral. Throughout the cruise, they pause at every table frequently, promoting and instilling a sense of concern and good cheer that they hope, on the last night, will prompt receipt of a coveted envelope.

Regardless, many passengers ignore them completely. Captains are more inclined to receive tips, simply because they remain in daily contact with their tables, able to produce special treats on demand, perhaps a special salad or pasta or a flambé dessert. This day-to-day exposure is denied the roaming maître d'hôtel. "What's he ever done for me?" is the not-unfamiliar response when it is suggested that passengers tip the man in charge of the dining room. In any event, if you wish to tip either man, $10 apiece is perfectly appropriate. I recommend strongly that, on your last night, you tip your maître d'hôtel either the moment you enter the dining room or at least the moment you first see him; later that evening, he may well be off foraging elsewhere. Your sommelier or wine waiter, if there is one, derives a 15% automatic gratuity from each charge slip so you are not obliged to tip him further.

Tipping horror stories abound, from passengers who disembark without leaving a penny behind (the British brand them "walk-offs") to those who try getting away with as little as possible. A Royal Caribbean steward shared a cruel shortfall he once experienced. Three little old ladies, retired schoolteachers on their first cruise, woefully misinterpreted the vessel's tip sheet: Enclosed with an effusive note of thanks in each of their envelopes were three crisp dollar bills, the recommended daily tip. Each had mistakenly assumed the amount covered their dining room obligation for the entire cruise.

On a Royal Viking ship some years ago, a perennial complainer carped ceaselessly about his food—the steak was too rare, the mashed potato lumpy and, time and time again, the coffee too cold. On the last morning, he demanded a hotter pot of coffee. When the steward, anxious to please, raced back from the galley, he found that his most troublesome passenger had disembarked, leaving him with no tip at all.

(The story has a nice sequel. Two years later, the steward was on a train in Switzerland, chatting with a chum who worked in the dining car. On his way back to his seat, he passed a first-class compartment with one occupant, the same passenger who had stiffed him aboard ROYAL VIKING SEA. Seizing the moment, the steward ran back to the dining car, borrowed a waiter's jacket and returned to the compartment bearing a tray with a cup of coffee. He knocked, entered and bowed low: "Here's your coffee, sir," he murmured ingratiatingly. "I'm sorry it took me so long to bring it." My only refinement would have been to invert tray and contents onto the passenger's lap.)

In an attempt to increase their take, some dining room stewards try priming the passenger pump, dwelling longingly on the impending arrival of a new baby or the larger apartment that addition to the family will entail. Personally, I feel that kind of transparent manipulation is a mistake; most passengers see through it and are turned off. At the same time, however, though some passenger/steward affection may be contrived to encourage larger tips, much is genuine. The cordiality between the dining room staff and the passengers they have indulged can be genuinely moving; I am no longer surprised to see the hugs, kisses and fond endearments exchanged between stewards and their female admirers at the moment of final departure from the dining room.

Tipping is, perforce, shrouded in mystery because it is impossible to track whether passengers adhere to or exceed the suggested scale. The amount sealed within every envelope remains, as it should be, utterly confidential. So too, the sum total contained in those envelopes when stewards tear them open in the privacy of their quarters remains privileged information. I have sometimes wondered—and will never find out—how much in tips a maître d'hôtel who has assiduously worked every table aboard a megaship takes home each week. Even if he were to average no more than a dollar apiece from approximately 3000 passengers, he will receive substantial supplementary income.

Aboard upscale vessels, tipping has been completely abolished. Ships of the Silversea, Seabourn and Sea Goddess lines, for example, state clearly and unequivocally in company literature that tips of any kind are not only not expected, they will also be refused. This, together with free drinks and better food, explains the high per diems these luxurious vessels command. Stewards must be paid a commensurate living wage that makes their non-tipped employment supportable and they know, when signing on, that they cannot expect any additional passenger income.

Aboard Seabourn vessels, a sensible tipping option has been established. If passengers feel compelled to demonstrate financial gratitude, they are invited to contribute to a shipboard welfare fund that specifically underwrites crew recreation—athletic equipment, sporting events and occasional barbecues or outings ashore.

Aboard Renaissance cruise ships, there is perpetual open sitting in every one of the vessel's restaurants. To ensure equitable distribution of tips to both waiters and cabin stewards, it is recommended that passengers contribute $15 per passenger per day to a ship-wide pool, funds that will be distributed to the appropriate recipients by the purser. Thanks to that fixed, promulgated figure, the company invites passengers to pre-pay their entire tip budget when booking passage. This has the effect of obviating any awkwardness or embarrassment in Renaissance dining rooms at cruise's end for, truth to tell, many passengers far prefer to have the business of tipping out of their hands, taken care of before they embark.

Lodged enigmatically between the megaships' tipped stewards

and the miniships' non-tipped, are the smiling Indonesians and Filipinos who serve as cheerful company servants throughout Holland-America Line's fleet. The company advertises proudly in their literature that they espouse a fleet-wide "tipping not required" policy. Regardless of that staff decision made by generals far behind the lines, perception among NCOs and privates manning the company trenches is markedly different. At cruise's end, when push comes to shove, Holland-America's black-and-white "no tipping required" rule turns disconcertingly telltale gray. Although no envelopes are disseminated, cruise directors delivering their disembarkation talks must straddle a fine line, paying dutiful lip service to the party line while in the next breath, encouraging passengers—*only if they would like*—to tip stewards generously. Most do, I sense, only because they feel compelled to.

This disparity is puzzling, to my mind, double-speak separating promise from performance that the company might do well to reconsider. Though Holland-America publicly disparages tipping, they do not, unlike Silversea or Seabourn, forbid it. But it seems to me that the company cannot have it both ways; either their no tipping disclaimer should be renounced or enforced. The present hair-splitting only confuses or, more likely, irritates unsuspecting Newpax.

In sum, tipping at sea is, for better or worse, a reality, inextricably entwined with shipboard. Yet in truth, be aware that tipping anyone on board a cruise ship is completely your decision. If you are prepared to tough it out, determined to spend no more than your price of passage, that remains your undoubted privilege. But you should be aware that the major portion of every steward's income depends on passenger tips. Yet again, in support of this time-honored but frequently maligned practice, let me repeat my considered opinion that a tipped steward is a more dedicated steward.

The fourth epigraph at the head of this chapter, quoting my SAGAFJORD fellow passenger who wondered if the crew lived on board, does in fact illumine a profound truth. Not only does the crew live on board, the vessel is their home in a way that most of us seldom appreciate. Whereas passengers are transitory shipboard tenants, the crew stays on board cruise after cruise. We come and go, they remain; we are visitors, they are inhabitants. Legitimate owners notwithstanding, the vessel belongs in a very real sense to its resident occupants. They exist within an alternate, bustling arena below that duplicates and distends, like fun-house mirrors at a carnival, the more sedate to-and-fro of passenger life permeating the upper decks.

Theirs is a backstage world of echoing steel staircases, frenetic activity, late nights and cabins crowding the waterline, a life that passengers never observe, let alone penetrate. Indeed, two great divides cleave the shipping world: The logistical gulf separating ships from headquarters ashore and, just as pronounced, that peculiarly unbridgeable gulf separating passengers from crew.

The social tempo throughout the crew's world functions nonstop. Not on board to play, they are there to work, intensively hard. Whatever recreation they enjoy must dovetail with the unforgiving span of their working hours. Consequently, crew social life hums well into the night. And whatever entertainment is devised to amuse the passenger body each evening, that unseen hive of activity beyond the green baize door far exceeds it.

I have been made aware, too often, just how all-consuming crew night life is. Over the years, cruise staff, shop assistants, assistant pursers and stewards often lament that they wish they could hear one of the illustrated lectures I deliver to passengers every sea day. Through the crew purser or welfare officer, a formal request is made for me to do a special talk for the crew, scheduled after midnight in

A stewardess trio aboard CRYSTAL HARMONY enjoys a rare moment in the sun. Indubitably, the ship belongs to the crew.
Barry M. Winiker

one of the public rooms, after passengers have either gone to bed or are engaged elsewhere.

Though I always comply with those requests, in almost every instance, it is a decision I regret. The turnout is invariably minimal, an audience of perhaps two dozen scattered about a lounge designed to accommodate several hundred. Compounding the irritation, conspicuously (and gallingly) absent are many of the same people who had begged me to give the talk in the first place. These no-shows are always apologetic, explaining that on the night in question, there had been an unexpected birthday party or anniversary or farewell party or welcome aboard party—in short, an irresistible gathering below stairs that preempted their attendance. Something compelling is *always* going on down in crew country, non-stop celebratory distraction that takes precedence over everything else on board.

The hotel staff in particular spend their working days and evenings in what can become grating proximity to the passenger body. This is total immersion, a 7/24 stint, with no restorative weekends intruding. A change of passenger-load makes little difference; the beat goes on. On duty, the men and women of the crew must adhere to strict company expectations, always smiling, always courteous, always dispensing advice, help and good cheer. That concerned regime prevails throughout the vessel. A bar waitress recognizes an habitué and recommends a favorite cocktail; the maître d'hôtel schmoozes with diners as he circulates around the dining room; a deck steward reminisces—perhaps more fondly than he feels—with a passenger encountered from a previous cruise; an assistant purser tries to clarify, maybe for the third time, the intricacies of a shipboard form to an anxious passenger; a casino dealer exchanges badinage with a regular at his table. And, particularly on the first days of the voyage, everyone from lowliest cleaner to chief purser will patiently point a lost passenger in the right direction to a lounge or dining room destination.

Sustaining that unfailingly courteous facade can be wearing. Sometimes those fixed smiles and cheery rejoinders come at a price. More than a few passengers are unreasonable or demanding, many a little dim, a few incomprehensible, others painfully talkative, some dangerously combative. And the need to handle the normal, as well as the senile, volatile or obstreperous elements of the passenger corpus, demands a high degree of dedicated professionalism. I often think that young crew members must feel they are coping for much of their day with tiresome parent or grandparent stand-ins.

The boundaries of crew concern were once abruptly delineated to me years ago aboard or, rather, alongside FRANCE. At the end of a westbound crossing, I was waiting on the lower level of Pier 88 to extricate my disembarked station wagon from the clutches of the U.S. Department of Agriculture before driving it home to my Manhattan garage. As I waited for some elusive document to be delivered, two senior men from the purser's department strolled by, bound for shore and clad in civilian clothes rather than their sober French Line livery. Though the soul of respectful congeniality on board earlier that morning, the two scarcely acknowledged me. Out of uniform and off the FRANCE, the game was over, passenger niceties curtailed. The French Line's impeccable concern ended at the gangway. It was a lesson, once learned, that I have never forgotten.

Similarly, over the years, Mary and I are often invited to crew parties on board. Though flattered to be asked and made ostensibly welcome, we inevitably feel ourselves outsiders as that inevitable divide separating passenger from crew prevails. Though we know most staff aboard many cruise ships and though ostensibly employed by the company, we are not really crew. (Similarly, we are not really passengers but unique hybrids that defy easy classification.) And however we try blending in, we are never completely successful. The adamantine bonds linking the crew have been annealed within a relentless shipboard crucible over thousands of sea days and sea miles, of interminable hours of patient duty, of crew lifeboat drills, of crowding and camaraderie, of pressured regulation and behavior. However welcomed, intruders never belong.

This is not to say that all crew/passenger symbiosis is necessarily doomed. For younger Nonpax in particular, the opportunity to meet and enjoy various members of the ship's company is a cruising given. Countless lifelong relationships have been initiated by preliminary meetings aboard a cruise ship.

Herewith the story of a shipboard marriage quite obviously

made in heaven that began with a chance passenger/crew encounter at sea. Diane Parker works as a hair stylist in Fallbrook, California. As one of a large family party hosted by her stepfather, she embarked for her first cruise aboard the original SUN PRINCESS in May 1982. Sailing out of San Juan, the Parker tribe was bound for a fortnight's cruise through the Panama Canal that would carry them back to California.

On the second evening, the night of the captain's reception, Diane went to the ship's discotheque. There, she met Alan Wadham, a handsome 27-year-old Englishman who served as one of the vessel's junior electrical officers. They met, danced, talked and, by evening's end, had become firm friends.

Diane told me recently that since the SUN PRINCESS's passenger load for that cruise tended to be elderly, young passengers were in a distinct minority. As a result, it was not surprising that every Parker sibling made friends among the crew. Diane, of course, had met Alan; one sister paired up with a ship's musician, another with a waiter, a third with a bartender and so on. (That vessel of the love boat fleet quite obviously lived up to its descriptive!)

Casual shipboard liaisons of this kind are common, customarily ending at the moment of passenger disembarkation. As it happened, after SUN PRINCESS reached her destination, she was due immediately for a three-day wet dock in San Pedro. Diane's mother, knowing that most of her children's shipboard friends would be at liberty, hosted a large dinner party at the Parker household in nearby Fallbrook.

Ironically, the only man with no time off and hence unable to attend was electrical officer Alan Wadham. Regardless, contact was sustained because after dinner, Diane arranged cleverly to drive the shipboard contingent back to San Pedro; thanks to their help, she was able to re-embark and see Alan again.

Within a flurry of serpentines, the master welcomes the newly-married Wadhams on board.
Diane Wadham

Over the next three years, the couple kept in touch by mail and telephone. It was not lost on Diane that her stepfather, Bob Switzer, had declared himself an instant admirer of Alan. Indeed, moments after he was introduced to the young Englishman, Bob whispered conspiratorially to his stepdaughter: "That boy is marriage material," an obviously prescient observation.

When Alan next had time off in California, he visited the Switzer/Parker family in Fallbrook and, shortly thereafter, Diane flew to England to meet Alan's mother. By then, Alan had proposed, Diane had accepted and a California wedding was arranged to take place in May 1985, almost three years to the day since the night of the couple's first meeting aboard ship.

They were married in Long Beach's First Congregational Church and the reception was held—where else?—in the International Lounge aboard SUN PRINCESS, once again laid up for a convenient three-day wet dock in San Pedro. The guest list was almost exclusively Californian; only Alan's mother and another English couple had flown out from the U.K. After leaving the church, the newlyweds drove to the pier at the head of a cavalcade of 450 guests. The bridal couple led the way up the gangway beneath an arch of oars held up by the vessel's rowing team and were pelted with streamers and serpentines by their friends. They were welcomed on board by Captain Malcolm Rushen and his officers before dancing began in the International Lounge.

A portion of the Wadhams' month-long honeymoon to follow was, in effect, a busman's holiday. After spending a week on their own in Santorini, they flew to Athens and joined PACIFIC PRINCESS for a two-week cruise to Rome. As of this writing, the Wadhams have been happily married for 14 years. Since a recent promotion awarded him three-and-a-half stripes, Alan has unlimited opportunity to have Diane with him on board. Although they do not maintain a shoreside domicile in Britain, they have bought a house in Fallbrook. Diane still retains her position as what she is careful to describe as an "independently contracted" hair stylist; the distinction is important because the flexibility of her employment enables her to join Alan at sea whenever she wishes. He serves now as Chief Electro-Technical officer aboard GRAND PRINCESS.

Their continuing shipboard idyll together is vastly simplified in that they have made the decision not to have children; thus, they continue to spend large portions of the year sailing together. Diane has discovered that when husbands leave the sea, opting for work ashore, formerly happy crew marriages can go sour.

The Wadhams' marriage is, in fact, atypical. Most ship's officers and their subordinate crews are raising families and can no longer pursue the same carefree life. The sea is a hard master and the extended absences of fathers who work aboard ship create understandable stresses, let alone sadness, in thousands of crew marriages. Husbands and wives with growing families must endure continual separations, during which the mother raises the children alone for long portions of every year. Fathers returning home after six-months' absence are often perceived as strangers by children too young to remember their last leave.

Let me touch again on the special fondness stewards exhibit for children. Many's the time I have invited young nephews or nieces on board for lunch; invariably, they are outrageously indulged by every steward in the dining room. In truth, those young passenger/visitors serve as transparent surrogates for the stewards' own, sorely-missed children at home.

Apart from their stewards, crew members with whom passengers enjoy the most daily contact are the cruise staff. Their chief is the cruise director, the vessel's incontestable master of revels. It is he—or occasionally she—who mingles congenially among the passengers, who edits the vessel's invaluable daily program, whose voice is heard making announcements over the loudspeaker, who schedules and introduces every evening's entertainment and who routines tender service to shore when the vessel is anchored out. In the event a port has to be passed up, it is the cruise director who must improvise a schedule of daytime activities for that unanticipated, additional sea day. Most cruise directors are talented performers themselves, either with a musical background as instrumentalist and singer or, inevitably, a dab hand at impromptu standup.

The cruise staff remains in evidence all over the vessel, dressed in distinctive uniforms and eminently approachable to proffer directions, advice or good cheer. Assistant cruise directors cope with all

In a cruise ship lounge, an off-duty steward indulges a visiting baby.
Author's Collection

manner of passenger diversions, from circulating daily passenger quizzes to checking books out of the library. When the weather is good, they officiate at nonsense games around the swimming pool or, when the weather is bad, organize indoor putting competitions. Children's playrooms and areas are under the supervision of extremely personable and competent cruise staff who ensure that every small and not-so-small passenger has a fun-filled cruise that is the equivalent of their parents'.

It is the cruise line's fervent hope that their parents' cruise lives up to expectation as well and, in that regard, an infallible litmus test remains at its disposal. At the conclusion of every voyage, passengers are encouraged to vent their opinions, offering candid input about every on-board service to which they have been exposed. They do so on specially devised comment cards that appear under cabin doors.

Comment cards serve, in effect, as each cruise's unvarnished report card, soliciting passenger opinion about everything that happened throughout the voyage. Under review are the dedication and skill of the stewards, the taste and presentation of the food, the caliber of the entertainment, the success of the shore excursions, the cleanliness of cabins, corridors and public rooms and the performance of the cruise staff. In addition to those multiple choice responses, a blank page is incorporated for those who wish, in longhand, to document any specific complaints or commendations of which they feel management should be made aware.

Comment cards are immensely valuable to the cruise lines, timely fingers on the service pulse throughout their fleets. Most passengers fill them out conscientiously and to encourage them, some cruise lines offer door prizes to be drawn on the last morning from submitted comment cards.

Alongside the pier, sealed boxes of completed cards are collected from the lobby to be screened and tabulated ashore by weekend staffs of temporary help. Especially aboard ships sailing in and out of Floridian ports, comment cards cast an immediate, ubiquitous shadow. It has been said at Royal Caribbean's pier-side Miami office that complaints about cold coffee, a bad salad or staff rudeness are absorbed ashore even before passengers have begun disembarking. As a result, the offending steward or sous-chef can be called to account before the vessel sails that afternoon and the problem remedied. Comment cards from ships overseas require a longer response time but their impact carries equal weight.

Passenger comments are taken very seriously. In fact, shipboard promotions (and, occasionally, demotions) depend on cumulative ratings that individual crew members garner week after week. Low or disappointing ratings for a particular cruise distress masters, hotel managers and cruise directors alike; was it merely bad weather or did the crew at large or in part fail to live up to company expectations?

I shall close this long crew chapter with a cautionary ship-to-shore tale told me long ago by a retired cruise director. In the early days, on vessels carrying first-time passengers to the Caribbean, the fount of all shipboard wisdom was the cruise director. Before arrival in every port, he would address passengers in the lounge, offering specific shopping, swimming and sightseeing recommendations, advice that was always accepted with innocent enthusiasm and trust.

Several cruises earlier, the cruise director had lunched at a good but under-patronized seafood restaurant along a remote stretch of St. Maarten beach. Though the lobster was good, business was obviously bad and the cruise director suggested an arrangement: He would steer multitudes of passengers there for lunch every Wednesday and, in return, the lobsterman would pay him a bounty of two dollar per passenger.

So, as part of his next St. Maarten lecture, the cruise director extolled the gastronomic virtues of the little lobster shack with the result that the place was overrun. The patron made money and, to a lesser extent, so did the cruise director.

But after a few months, the restaurateur suggested to his wife: "We're on the map now; no need to pay that guy any more." He abrogated the agreement, advising the cruise director that their deal was off.

The following week, the cruise director's St. Maarten briefing incorporated a special caveat, warning his passengers about a particular lobster shack where, he cautioned them darkly, several passengers on previous cruises had eaten and become extremely unwell. Needless to say, Wednesday business at the lobster shack plummeted. Within a fortnight, the agreement had been renegotiated, the cruise director's cut now three dollars a head.

That particular gulf between ship and shore was, for a time, uneasily bridged.

CHAPTER X

Delights

Never a ship sails out of the bay
But carries my heart as a stowaway.

—Roselle Mercier Montgomery, *The Stowaway*

I do not wonder men see you as women—
You in the white length of your loveliness
reclining on the sea!

—Sally Bruce Kinsolving, *Ships*

It is my hope that the mother lode of shipboard minutiae unearthed between these covers responds to every conceivable Nonpax query. By way of perhaps needless amplification, herewith some personal shipboard likes and dislikes, categorized in successive chapters of Delights and Horrors.

One of my fondest shipboard pleasures, for example, occurs just as we leave the dock. You will always find me lurking somewhere along the promenade deck railing. "Standing up for the kickoff" is the way I characterize my departure to Mary as she continues unpacking and putting our cabin to rights.

Though I have probably duplicated that anticipatory vigil hundreds of times, the lure persists. I am not alone in my preoccupation; it is shared by other departure fanatics, maritime sidewalk superintendents all. Each has laid claim to a foot or two of accommodating teak, lost in thought as the ritual plays out below. My neighbors are unknowns, fellow inhabitants of a ship filled momentarily with strangers, fellow passengers not yet coalesced. And without fail, along those railings, first tentative overtures will be exchanged.

Gazing down at the pier, we watch as a dockside crane grinds to a halt amidships. Stevedores rig slings and the gangway is lofted up, rocking gently on its suspended pivot point like an empty seesaw, before being lowered back to earth alongside the pier shed, against the day of the next arrival. The last of embarkation's set pieces have been removed, final shore escape shunted into oblivion.

Above, the ship's whistle blasts impatiently, momentarily overwhelming a combo of ship's musicians who tootle gamely nearby. Cruise staff has distributed rolled serpentines to those who wish and many of my neighbors hurl those vibrant, spiraling links to wherever they can. Some reach the concrete, some come to rest in the crane's jib, others merely festoon our railings. Caught up in the drama of separation, passengers wave at perfect strangers on the dock who always wave back eagerly. Small children make the most satisfactory spectators at a sailing because they are so visibly pleased, so enchanted by the giant ship that they literally dance with pleasure.

But those familiar dockside manifestations are of less appeal to me than the more subtle moment of departure that follows almost at once. As a widening water gap separates pier from hull, the episodic turmoil of bow- and stern-thrusters ceases; crab-like sideways drift is supplanted by cautious forward motion. By walking aft at the same speed as the ship, passengers can apparently neutralize their progress.

Now we are gathering speed, bows pointed toward harbor exit. We are under cautious way, privileged tenants within a benign, kinetic enclosure, all shore fixtures but one erased: the pilot, still on our bridge but shortly to disembark, remains the sole alien who cannot qualify as permanent soul on board.

Over the years, I have struggled in vain to find just the right word to describe a ship's in-harbor movement, every voyage's tentative first step. Out at sea, my task will be easier—the vessel may plunge, creak, heave, roll, labor, steam or just sail. In harbor, newly-detached from the pier, the ship starts "moving" implacably towards the breakwater. But the word "moving" cannot begin to characterize our preliminary displacement to sea. Do we glide, slide or creep across those harbor waters? Despite English's normally florid resources, *le mot juste*—describing that stately, majestic, awe-inspiring progression—simply does not exist. It seems ironic that this perennial cruising delight should prove so indescribable.

Of course, what I also find captivating about that particular moment involves more than the ship's movement. We are witness to the shrugging-off of land, to a resumption of sea-going purpose, to that sense of ship, crew and passengers girding themselves for the nascent voyage to come.

Unless there is an extraordinary sunset in train, the decks become gradually deserted and underfoot, one can feel the first gentle motion. As I descend to my cabin, stewards with vacuum cleaners strapped to their backs are scouring every last vestige of shoreside litter from staircase and corridor carpeting. Another delight, shared, I am sure, by those who struggle as I do to keep dwellings dust free, is shipboard's unrelenting campaign against dirt, whether litter, dust, grime, handprint, stain, smudge or smear. It is a curious fact of life that passengers cannot resist touching the signs designed to inform them, many of which incorporate brass or glass. Not only are smudges endemic to shipboard signage, some of their letters will be literally obliterated by successive hundreds of passenger fingers.

Years ago, aboard Holland-America ships, the task of vacuuming staircases was always scheduled during low-traffic periods, when passengers had either gone ashore or to bed. But one canny Dutch housekeeper surmised, correctly, that passengers would prefer seeing their vessel maintained at spotless perfection before their eyes. So now vacuum cleaners are at work throughout days and evenings aboard all cruise ships, regardless that passengers moving up and down staircases have to negotiate over or around trailing electric cords.

But it is more than carpeting that receives all that scrupulous attention. A ceaseless cleaning regime pervades the vessel, indoors and out, around the clock. Paneling is wiped down, brass polished, chrome buffed, windows and glass doors squeegeed crystal clear. On the top decks, cleaners with brushes and soap remove stains and spills from deck chairs and tables. Painters from the deck gang keep the superstructure's white gleaming and maintain every railing top's sinuous, varnished perfection. Chairs and sofas are inspected for the slightest wear and any sign of faded, sagging or worn fabric merits instant dispatch down to the vessel's upholsterers for replacement.

Our pristine floating environment celebrates, with a vengeance, the dedication of seemingly unlimited reserves of ship's manpower, strong, willing crew in comforting numbers turning their hand to long-prescribed tasks. For example, whenever special buffets are mounted either in a lounge or out on deck, tables, cloths, crockery, silver, flowers, ice sculptures and ornately decorated platters materialize on cue, assembled and arrayed well before time, awaiting the inevitable passenger onslaught. This is the well-oiled, flawless machinery of the vessel's hotel side at work. Cleanliness, order and calm are shipboard's watchwords and I always revel in our gleaming, burnished surround that retains its luster day after day.

I enjoy shipboard music enormously, especially that increasingly supplied by string trios or quartets. Sounds of Mozart, Strauss or Kreisler, echoing up from the depths of an atrium, permeate everywhere and bring back fond recollections of countless teatime concerts aboard ocean liners past. It is the strings that do it, those haunting, civilized strains so perfectly attuned to one's automatic evocation of shipboard. For me, the pleasure of an evening's piano recital in a lounge is always enriched by the sea's juxtaposition. There is something exquisitely apropos about a well-rendered Chopin étude accompanied by its shipboard obligato of gently heaving deck or minuscule tremor of a glass table top.

One of the most interesting interfaces between ship and music is emphasized each time I enjoy breakfast in bed aboard QE2. On my television set, thanks to the bridge's forward-facing camera, I can watch our bow persevering across a typically blustery North Atlantic seascape. A classical music track habitually accompanies the image. I always find it fascinating that whatever the random musical selection—whether the crisp precision of a Bach sonata or a sonorous chestnut from a Beethoven symphony—it always provides the perfect aural counterpoint for the vision of our relentless transatlantic quest. Music and the sea belong together, the creak of cabin bulkhead marrying perfectly with the strings' plaintive threnody.

One ancient delight that remains, alas, an elusive chimera aboard every one of today's cruise ships is a barbershop. A century and a

Lament for shipboard's *tonsor evanescatus,* the vanished barber: Two passengers avail themselves of a haircut aboard Hamburg America's IMPERATOR. *Author's Collection*

half ago, the American Collins liner BALTIC, driven by sails as well as steam, boasted the North Atlantic's first, complete with a rotating, elevating chair. The owners of every new ship always try to incorporate a special gimmick with which to tickle the press; without question, BALTIC's novel fixture did the trick in 1851.

Soon, imitative barbershops appeared aboard every liner. Moreover, the barber was permitted to supplement his tonsorial income by the sale of sundries, postcards and trinkets. As a result, long before companies provided on-board shops of their own, his establishment served as a magnet for early passenger shoppers.

But nowadays, the barbershop, the barber chair and, saddest of all, the barber himself have disappeared. When asked by Royal Caribbean as well as Cunard whether I had any suggestions for either VOYAGER OF THE SEAS or Cunard's QUEEN MARY 2 project respectively, at the top of my list was the urgent recommendation that this vanished gentleman's fixture be resuscitated. Nowadays, male passengers in quest of a shipboard haircut must make an appointment with a member of the beauty salon's staff—customarily but not always female—whose specialité, I have found, may be hair dressing or hair styling but seldom hair cutting.

It is not lost on me that, in agitating for the return of the male barber, I am negotiating a precarious sexist minefield, fraught with hair-trigger detonations of political incorrectness, gender blindness or the dread chauvinism. But bear with me. Men dislike entering beauty salons and submitting to the scented ministrations of a distracted barberette. Similarly, they dislike being seated uneasily on a rolling chair with a collapsible back within a patently feminine enclave, immersed in the chatty camaraderie of the salon's habituées. Far better the masculine ministration of a skilled barber within a sober, paneled ambience. Moreover, within the ship's geography, that barbershop should be sited along a well-traveled passenger thoroughfare so that men can drop by—once again, on impulse if necessary. One day, barbers will go back to sea and I shall be there.

High among my perennial shipboard delights is the probability of the impromptu. At home, bent on errand or duty, chance meetings with friends involve little more than a hasty greeting en passant. But aboard ship, where we all march to the same languid drummer, chance encounters bear unexpected fruit, turning effortlessly into a mutually agreeable pause for coffee, a drink or even a meal together. This scenario of impulse, of amending one's schedule on a whim, remains a cherished shipboard perquisite.

And, last but certainly not least among shipboard delights, I relish the opportunity of being in the top deck pool when the ship encounters long ocean swells. Nothing is more pleasurable than swimming or, at least, floating under these auspicious circumstances. You must be lucky enough to experience just the right intensity of pitching, pronounced enough to deliver a slam-bang, tsunami effect yet not serious enough to oblige the bosun to drain the pool.

All shipboard pools are girdled with either a belt of wave-absorbing baffles or, more usual, a surrounding dyke, so that water sloshing out of the pool stays within its confines rather than flooding the adjacent deck. As soon as the pool's repetitive wave patterns—miniatures, in fact, of the full-sized versions encountered by the bow far below—begin their pendulum effect, get into the water and, literally, ride the waves. Impressive, watery undulations sweep the length of the pool, both forward and aft, all of which you surmount with sublime indifference. Contrary to expectations, you will never be dashed against the pool ends but will remain happily afloat within a protective cushion of roiled water. Many passengers (predominantly children) and I have been known to spend hours within that exhilarating flume, the envy of reluctant spectators.

Of course, if the seas become really disorganized, if the pool must be drained, if air sick bags appear outside elevators or, God forbid, lines are strung across lobbies, then our barograph of shipboard enjoyment may flicker into the nether portion of the dial, Delights transmogrified into Horrors. Merely turn the page and you are there.

CHAPTER XI

Horrors

If you want to learn to pray, go to sea.

—Ancient Portuguese sailor's proverb

Researchers have now established that motion sickness occurs when there is a conflict between the motion we experience and the motion we expect to experience.

—Atul Gawande, *A Queasy Feeling in The New Yorker*

Sorry for the bumps. You must realize that we find ourselves on the bosom of the ocean; and bosoms, as you all know, are occasionally inclined to heave.

—The late Commodore John Young

I was initially hesitant about including a chapter titled thus, even buried near the end of *Cruise Savvy*. But so many potential passengers dread the specter of seasickness that I thought it wise to bite the bullet with a frank discussion about this traditional shipboard nemesis. I like to think that cruising has no downside but if there is one—and mind you, only a very slight one—it might be seasickness.

Additionally, to lay this chapter's course on the line, I plan to share some personal shipboard negatives as well, passing from uncomfortable sea motion to discomfiting passenger or company motion, all of which I have taken the liberty of including under the comprehensive rubric Horrors.

First, let us examine seasickness, *mal de mer* to the French and *Seekrankeit* for the Germans. Charles Dickens, felled during a winter crossing aboard BRITANNIA in 1842, recorded the sufferer's definitive symptom: "Not ill, but going to be." Aboard today's cruise ships, we can adapt and update that pronouncement to "Not ill, and not likely to be." By way of reassurance to the Non-pax, there exist so many excellent counter-measures with which to combat seasickness that, to my mind, the ancient scourge has been, if not quite eradicated, certainly neutralized. There are injections of Promethazine, there are scapolamine patches, worn proudly behind the ear, there are suppositories worn surreptitiously elsewhere and there are always pills containing dimenhydrinate.

This latter started life as an experimental antihistamine. Blind tests of the drug were being conducted in Baltimore during the late 1940s. On a weekly basis, patients swallowed either a placebo or dimenhydrinate to assess its performance during the allergy season. One woman who came in from the suburbs for her regular dose, reported coincidentally to the doctors that although the ride *into town* on the streetcar invariably made her seasick, she always felt fine on the return journey. Dimenhydrinate, it turned out, was far more efficacious against motion sickness than allergies, and, under the brand name Dramamine, entered the formerly barren pharmacopoeia of the distressed voyager by sea, plane or car, grand specific for that unhappy affliction.

Incidentally, you should never feel a particle of shame in seeking out any of the excellent medicinal remedies obtainable on board. Throughout the trembling ranks of the seasick susceptible, no medals for bravery are or ever have been awarded. Dr Eilif Dahl, a staunch Norwegian ship's surgeon who is as dotty about cruising as I am, once published a pioneering study, long overdue, about seasickness, a subject that cruise lines understandably prefer to soft pedal. Following one passenger survey that his employing company reluctantly permitted him to conduct, Eilif encountered one pervasive statistic. Male passengers in particular exhibited a stubborn, macho reluctance to succumb, as they perceived it, to medicinal relief; apparently, they thought it manlier to try and tough it out for too long before taking a pill or donning a patch. Remember, there are no medals…

Moreover, it is not inevitable that you will be affected by seasickness. There seems no way to predict who will or will not get seasick—some do while at least as many do not. No one to my knowledge has yet devised a formula identifying those who may be predisposed to the condition. A late nineteenth century psychologist, William James, ascertained that certain deaf people—but not all, apparently—did not suffer any ill effects from sea motion.

That auditory clue is scarcely surprising for it is deep within the inner ear that the dread symptom is initially triggered. In a receptor structure, the *crista ampularis*, there are growths of delicate hairs; when disturbed by abrupt, unanticipated or disorienting motion, they transmit their confusion to the brain which proceeds immediately to alert the stomach; hence, the nauseating effects of seasickness. Wouldn't you know that the ancient Greek word for ship was nausea?

Surprisingly, the most effective cure for seasickness, although unavailable from druggist or physician, is delivered gratis to us all in the fullness of time. This, the ultimate natural cure, accrues from the beneficial effects of aging. As we grow old, those inner ear hairs apparently lose their devilish motion sensitivity. Thus, increasing years bring with them an effective diminution of seasickness. That welcome, chronological dividend is, to my certain knowledge, one of the rare salutary benefits derived from growing older; it also may well account for the durable appeal of cruising among the retired.

There is another non-pharmaceutical approach to quelling seasickness, a pair of terrycloth bands wrapped tightly about each wrist, equipped with an in-facing stud that must be positioned to press on what is called the Nei-kuan point inside the forearm, an inch or two up the wrist.

Every floating object, whether aircraft carrier or length of driftwood, is subject in varying degrees to sea motion and aboard your cruise ship, there could be three different kinds of motion of which you will become aware. The first affects the vessel's fore and aft axis, a lift-and-fall of the bow which sailors call pitching, during which I repair at once to the pool. Pitching can occur with varying intensity. At its most serene, it is experienced as the majestic, up-and-down motion the bow makes when encountering long, almost imperceptible ocean swells. In fact, you may become so acclimated to this gentle motion that it is only when catching sight of the horizon at gentle variance with the benchmark of the ship's railing that you will realize it is happening at all.

At the other end of the pitching spectrum, if your ship is plowing into the teeth of a gale, the bow will rocket up to what seems, from your bunk, an incredible height. Then, after a moment's dithering hesitation, it will plunge back down atop an oncoming wave often with an audible and intrusive thump. To the uninitiated, that pronounced, repetitious thumping can be unnerving. When the Cresswells, our London chums, sailed on their first crossing through Hurricane Gloria aboard QUEEN ELIZABETH 2, John told me that he purposely kept his cabin television tuned to the bridge's remote camera, just to make sure, after each bang, that QE2's bow was still attached. Mary and I have become very familiar with those manic, pitching elevator rides near the bow for most cruise lines accommodate their lecturers in cabins located far forward.

The second distinctive motion you may encounter will be the hull rocking from side to side; this is called rolling. Although there is little any master can do to minimize pitching save slow down his vessel, he can reduce rolling almost to zero. Situated amidships on either side of the vessel are stabilizers, powerful steel fins that, when deployed on command from the bridge, project out from either side of the hull below the waterline.

Stabilizers are similar to and operate in precisely the same way as a whale's flippers. Once a built-in computer anticipates the severity of an expected roll, it sends instantaneous maneuvering commands to each stabilizer's powerful hydraulic muscle. Both fins are rotated appropriately to counter the sea's rolling effect and sustain the vessel's upright posture. It is very hard for passengers looking over the ship's side to actually see extended stabilizers because they are more likely to be deployed when seas are rough and consequently more or less opaque. But trust me, they will be in operation, a vital and efficient part of every modern cruise ship's motion-reducing arsenal. After a while, you will be able to sense the stabilizers' corrective surge whenever a roller approaches the side of the ship to little subsequent effect.

The third shipboard motion is a combination of pitching and

rolling which sailors identify as scending. Some but not all scending motion can be dampened by stabilizers; of the three, it is the most unpredictable and, if it persists, the most cumulatively exhausting.

Those of you who sail the Caribbean will find that for most of the year, its surface remains placid, a maritime testing ground in which beginner passengers can find, as they say, their sea legs. (Some sea legs remain damnably elusive. There are instances of admirals or career naval officers who are chronically susceptible to seasickness and never successfully overcome it; one can but admire their professional dedication.) Exceptions to the notorious Caribbean calm can take place either during the fall's hurricane season or occasionally in mid-winter, when Atlantic winter gales may extend their thrust through chinks in the Windward Island barrier. But for the most part, that traditional cruise playground remains ideally unruffled and so will you.

Be warned that apart from pills, patches or injections, there are amateur seasickness remedies to be had for the asking all over the vessel. They tend to be as ineffectual as they are numerous and, in my experience, are invariably promoted by those smug souls who never need them. Moreover, some seasickness cures prove contradictory; adhering to one recommended school of behavior may well run afoul of another. For example, retiring to bed in your cabin—my favorite remedy—obviously vitiates an opposing school of hearty sufferers for whom infusions of fresh air and exercise supposedly do the trick.

All ship's bartenders I've ever met have their own remedies, shaking up largely quack, alcoholic nostrums that invariably include brandy, port, blackberry cordial and ginger ale. Ginger in any form, it is reputed, helps alleviate seasickness although I am not convinced. Moreover—and here, once again, the rule of conflicting remedies comes into play—gulping down (assuming that you can swallow anything at all) strange concoctions flies in the face of those who insist on either a teetotal regime or nothing by mouth at all. Dry soda crackers are urged as a means of keeping something digestible in the stomach.

Having analyzed sometimes inescapable horror number 1, let me list 9 optional horrors in addition. As with all opinions expressed within these pages, those that follow are intensely personal, promulgated less to offend than to inform.

If seasickness is horror 1, horror 2 must be caps. An apparently irresistible item of clothing for male passengers, the baseball cap is equipped with an adjustable plastic size band at the back. Stitched or appliquéd above the visor is the name of the ship, a country club, an athletic team or, quite frequently, a purveyor of agricultural implements. These caps are unquestionably America's pop head-covering of choice.

My intent here is not to condemn my fellow passengers' choice of headgear, only to suggest they doff them when entering any ships' dining rooms; pray, as we used to say in the Marines, uncover. Some cruise ships have gone so far as to forbid caps at mealtimes and I can but applaud their rare temerity. For those of you who (a) are prone to caps and (b) embark aboard ships where the management has not yet drawn a haberdashery line, I urge you to don them on deck only.

Horror 3 also concerns caps: Is there any way to subvert the lamentable craze for wearing them backwards? I often wonder at the identity of the miscreant—Back-Cap One, we should call him—the high schooler who, either joking or defiant, first reversed his cap. Did he realize that his jape would develop into a late-century, in-your-face plague throughout the world? Some opportunistic manufacturers have accommodated Back-Cappers by stitching an alternative, miniature logo on the back of the cap so that it registers to the oncoming. I am never quite sure what Back-Cappers have going for them; for starters, worn thus in the sun, the practice offers a chilling medical preview, ratcheting up the odds for millions of melanoma to come.

Horror 4: This is a curious one that I see all the time. Let me urge you never to join the ranks of passengers who parade up and down staircases or into dining rooms carrying half-consumed drinks in their hands. Although it may speak well for their sense of economy, it does little for their image. Finish or, if necessary, abandon the drink where you ordered it and order another when you reach your destination; but please do not carry it with you.

Horror 5 is less horror than dreadful pity. One sees them on every ship, passengers who seem to have no inner resources whatsoever. They carry no books, knitting or needlepoint; they just sit and stare. And I am not necessarily talking about the lone, single passenger; sometimes couples just sit and stare. Though they talk very little to each other, they are only fractionally more loquacious with others and make few friends. In fact, they could just as well be anywhere but on a ship which seems to me brimful of tempting social opportunities.

Horror 6 is the use of a word that has become, through overuse, utterly meaningless. The word gourmet is a noun, describing someone who professes to be a connoisseur of good food. It makes a hopeless adjective; what exactly is gourmet dining? And at what point on an ascending gastronomic scale of either expertise or expense does a dish cross the threshold into gourmet land? Leave the word alone.

Horror 7 is another word, one increasingly employed among upscale cruise lines, to whit, substitution of the euphemism "guest" for "passenger." This false gentility is totally at odds with fact. Guests may inhabit hotels but very few embark aboard ships. Whereas passengers pay, guests never do. So unless those lines are trying to suggest that they embark freeloaders exclusively, I recommend they revert to passenger. It is an historically accurate and respectable word, usage as old as the sea. Though proud to be called passenger, I bridle at guest and hope you will too.

Horror 8 is really about courtesy. Many times, I have been corralled by open sitting into sharing a table with a dozen strangers. I am repeatedly struck how too many of them order three courses, consume them and leave the dining room without once saying please or thank you to the steward. You cannot thank your steward enough.

Horror 9? Not really a horror, more a lingering regret, the gradual disappearance of shipboard cinemas. Cabin television is partly to blame, though films screened throughout the day or night on that little box are no substitute for the pleasure of entering a shipboard cinema after dinner and sharing a film with your fellow passengers. The catastrophic erosion of shipboard projection—from 35 millimeter to the ubiquitous video cassette—is another sadness, quality sacrificed on the altar of convenience.

Horror 10 is one to which we are all subject, the grim prospect of final disembarkation. Indeed, there can be no better bridge into our final chapter.

CHAPTER XII

LANDFALL

"Good-bye! Farewell! See you soon!"
But, sadly, by mid-afternoon
A new and faceless client horde
Displaces us as souls on board.

—John Maxtone-Graham, *Crossing's End*

My mom just started her own business. She calls herself an "after-cruise consultant." What she does is for a small fee, she'll come over to your house after your cruise and look at your pictures and videos . . . and she'll pretend like she cares.

—Barnaby, shipboard juggler/comedian extraordinaire

The great French director, Francois Truffaut, always regretted the moment when he finished shooting a movie. Admittedly, the work was done and his film safely in the can. But he lamented the dispersal of his crew, that loyal family of experts who had helped nurse his vision into cinematic reality. As itinerant jobbers, they would soon sign on with different directors. Privately, Truffaut was saddened that *his* cameraman, *his* prop man, *his* focus-puller would now move on to other productions. Understandably if sentimentally, Truffaut thought of them as his special colleagues; unbearable was the thought that they might find contented employment elsewhere.

As final disembarkation looms, many of you will share the French director's sense of proprietary deprivation. Although on board for a comparatively short time, by cruise's end you will feel not only comfortably at home but loath to leave as well. You have long since mastered the vessel's geography, you move at ease about the public rooms and you have a host of new friends, among them the stewards who look after you in cabin, bar, pool or dining room. You and your ship will have achieved a hand-in-glove congeniality and it will distress you that, by mid-afternoon of the day you disembark, you will have been abruptly and unceremoniously replaced. "Your crew," to extend Truffaut's plaint, will be working for different passengers.

As you put out your suitcases in the corridor for the luggage team to transfer the following morning to the pier, do remember to retain clothing to wear off the ship, night things, toothbrush, razor etc. It is astonishing how many even experienced passengers, in their efficient rush to pack, sometimes neglect to retain necessities for their final hours on board.

You will find that on the morning of disembarkation, indifference characterizes formerly warm crew contacts. You have given them their tips and are about to leave the vessel, perhaps forever. However genial your just-completed cruising relationship, you will find that emotional shutters have come down and farewells, if any, are distant and off-hand.

It is not only the stewards, it is the entire shipload—officers, staff and even your fellow passengers. One voyage is over, another is imminent. While the entire crew is bracing itself for a new client onslaught, current passengers are preoccupied with luggage and flights. Indeed, from early that morning, you have become superannuated cargo, obliged to abandon your cabin, shoulder your belongings, eat breakfast and, as advised repeatedly by the ship's loudspeakers, "make yourself comfortable in one of the vessel's public rooms."

Throughout hundreds of disembarkations, I have never yet found it possible to derive comfort of any kind from public rooms that no longer belong to me. They are alien, impersonal spaces now, bereft of crew, the view through windows no longer sea or island but static pier shed. In truth, the reason pursers continually urge you into the public rooms is that they are anxious to disperse the determined, obstructing crowds of impatient passengers who, with the mistaken idea that it will somehow hasten their departure, crowd the gangway. Their vigil is, in effect, useless and you would do far better to take the purser's advice; all groups to be disembarked will be summoned in turn over the loudspeakers.

So you camp uneasily, distractedly, surrounded by hand luggage. The heavy stuff went out into the corridor last night and it is the chore of unloading those thousands of suitcases that keeps you fretting on board. There are only two exceptions to this inevitable delay, either those hearty souls who have somehow contrived to carry off everything they own—"self-help" is the euphemism—or passengers described as in-transit, booked for the subsequent cruise and able to go ashore in our final disembarkation port as mere day-trippers.

If you are returning to a United States port, customs and immigration inspectors troop on board and passengers must submit their passport for inspection. (For long transoceanic crossings, cruise lines often fly a brace of immigration inspectors to the foreign port of embarkation so that passenger and crew inspection can take place peacefully during the crossing. Those overseas chores are coveted among inspectors normally assigned to the hum-drum of airport or pier.) Those whose shopping indulgence has exceeded their $400 duty-free allowance are invited to settle up at this time. Luggage on the pier is seldom opened these days; the only scrutiny it undergoes is at the educated and addicted nose of a small dog that is led patiently up and down the lines of suitcases to sniff out any drugs.

That customs/immigration formality completed, there is little to do but return to your cache of luggage and wait. The ship's loudspeaker crackles to life repeatedly, summoning delinquent passengers to settle their accounts or present themselves to the immigration inspectors.

Once the ship has finally been cleared, the first consignment of airport passengers is summoned by loudspeaker; they gather up their belongings and head for the gangway. Once you are called ashore, you will enter a large luggage shed. Inside it, spread all over the floor, longshoremen have grouped your suitcases according to the color-coded tags distributed to cabins two days earlier. Locating and assembling luggage is almost easier than recruiting a porter to carry it out to the bus or taxi. (Am I right in assuming that it is these worthies who have prevented pier installation of the airport's ubiquitous luggage trolley?) Once ensconced within bus or taxi, you have only the airport ordeal in prospect, checking your luggage, getting to the gate and waiting (again) for your flight to depart. Fly, sail, fly—the cruise cycle has been completed.

Overall, the ordeal of disembarkation makes for an unpleasant, dispiriting day. You have exchanged carpet for concrete and the deferred responsibilities of home—bills, children, pets and lawns, so blithely abandoned just a short time ago—await your return. It is Mary's and my profound conviction that in addition to jet lag, there is cruise lag. Dawn awakening, packing, waiting to disembark and the prospect of re-embracing life ashore make for a cumulatively discomfiting experience, long before you clamber aboard your homebound aircraft.

If *you* hate disembarkations, cruise line marketing departments hate them even more. You succumbed to their advertised promise of the cruise, you bought your first ticket and nothing would please them more than to have you book another cruise with them. But the often negative experience of that disembarkation day, lumped with further possibilities of lost luggage, late or canceled flights and cranky taxi drivers, can sour things. However the cruise may have enchanted, its termination may well rankle, leaving a sour taste in the collective passenger mouth. Indeed, that single negative day can sometimes eclipse all the irreplaceable positives that flooded the preceding week. Hence, the company's parallel unhappiness. Sadly, I doubt there is any means of making the process less onerous. You must just resign yourself to a lost and dreary day, the ship and its passengers infected with an end-of-term bleakness, a recent joyful past relegated to memory and photographs.

Mary and I never say goodbye to anyone, whether passengers or crew, because we see so many of them again, either on the pier, at the airport or, most appropriately, months later aboard another vessel. And, of course, the prospect of boarding another ship does wonders for end-of-cruise distress. Cushion the blow of disembarkation by having a subsequent cruise already in mind. Incidentally, there is no better bargain than booking your next cruise while still on board. Most companies assign a marketing representative to their vessels who will be only too happy to sell you another cruise, which they will offer with a small discount for having been booked on board.

Now the dream is over and reality awaits. By way of genuine

Cruising's perfect panorama includes fellow passengers, ship, sun, island and, always, the beguiling sea. On the first day of her maiden voyage, MONARCH OF THE SEAS sails past Saba Island. *Author's Collection*

farewell, let me thank Nonpax who have persevered this far. I hope by now you will have absorbed sufficient cruise savvy to put newfound convictions to the test. Call your travel agent and book that first cruise; though there are few guarantees in life, I predict unequivocally that the pleasures to be derived from repeated infusions of shipboard will enchant you forever.

Cruising Glossary

Bollards Cast-iron, knobbed mooring devices set along the dock's concrete margins, over which hawser loops of incoming vessels are fixed.
Bridge Officer One of the junior officers from the deck department charged with manning the bridge, four hours on, eight hours off.
Bulkhead Nautical term for any shipboard wall or partition.
Bunkering The process of refueling the vessel, customarily with diesel oil. It is achieved in port alongside a small tanker.
Companionway Any ladder or staircase aboard ship.
Crossing A transoceanic voyage from one continent or coast to another, as opposed to an often circular cruise.
Cruise Director The most senior member of the cruise staff, charged with the scheduling and presentation for all passenger entertainment, amusement and recreation.
Deckhead Nautical term for any on-board ceiling.
Dry Dock A two-week maintenance ritual each vessel must undergo about every two years. The hull is removed from the water, scaled and repainted; anchor cables, rudders and propellers are checked at the same time. Any major structural refits are scheduled during dry docking as well.

Engineer The Chief Engineer and his staff are responsible for everything mechanical on board, from a cabin wall fan to all generators and propulsion motors.

Gangway The temporary walkway or bridge connecting vessel to pier during port calls. It is sometimes the property of the port, sometimes the ship's property and travels with the vessel. The crew customarily have their own gangway separate from the passengers.

Hawsers Long mooring lines, made of either hemp, nylon or occasionally wire cable, with which vessels are secured to the pier.

Hotel Manager The officer who heads the hotel side of the vessel, in charge of all stewards, cooks, musicians and entertainers. On some vessels, he or she is called the Chief Purser.

Lifeboat Drill A mandatory procedure that, according to maritime law, must take place within 24 hours of embarkation. All passengers are conducted to their lifeboat mustering stations and made familiar with wearing their lifejackets and the ship's safety regulations.

Master at Arms One of several crewmembers charged with maintaining shipboard security at the gangway as well as passenger and crew discipline.

Medical Center The ship's hospital, renamed thus to defer potentially litigious passengers. For reasons of improved stability, it is always located on the lowest possible passenger deck.

Newbuilding Shipyard shorthand for a newly constructed vessel, either throughout construction or about to be delivered to the owner.

Open Sitting Passenger meal service in a ship's dining room at which time no seats or tables are specifically reserved.

Out Island A small tropical island or length of beach, specifically designed for the disembarkation of passengers for a day's swimming, snorkeling and barbecue.

Purser The person in charge of payroll, papers and passenger manifests. A crew purser fulfills the same function for the entire crew.

Repositioning Crossing The transoceanic voyage that serves, each spring and fall, to relocate a cruise ship from its winter to summer market or the reverse. The voyage is invariably achieved with passengers on board. From Caribbean to Mediterranean would be a typical spring repositioning, as would from Caribbean to Alaskan waters.

Safety Officer A senior ship's officer charged with the outfitting and maintenance of all life-saving equipment.

Shell Plating The actual steel skin of the hull.

Shorex Customary cruise ship abbreviation for Shore Excursion.

Shuttle bus A bus or relay of busses employed to carry passengers back and forth from the pier to the port's downtown, sometimes complimentary, more often not.

Sittings One of two sequential meal services offered within the ship's passenger dining room.

Staff Captain The vessel's second-in command, charged with crew discipline and shipboard maintenance.

Steward Crew member assigned to be of personal service to passengers either in cabin, dining room, the bars or out on deck.

Transit Passenger A passenger who is not necessarily disembarking but remaining on board for a subsequent cruise.

Turnaround The generic process encompassing the homeport's end-of-cruise changeover of passenger loads and reprovisioning.

Wet Dock A vessel's brief layup at a pier in port for routine maintenance work such as re-carpeting, painting or minor construction.

INDEX

And the Ship Sails On, 16
AQUITANIA, 10, 60, 72
Atlantic Ferry, 11, 17

Balconies. See Cabin
BALTIC, 157
Barbershop, 156–58
Basch, Harry, 4
Beauty salon, 158
Berlitz Guide, 4
Bingo, 24, 100, 136
Boeing, 9
Boyer, Esther, 58
BREMEN, 11
Bridge, 110–11
BRITANNIA, 161
Burr, Lori, 99

Cabin, 63–70, 72–73; balconies, 68–71; bathroom, 65–66; key, 64; steward, 131–32, 136
Cairo, 116
Cape Cod Canal, 19–20
Captain's dinner, 92–93
Captain's Welcome Aboard Cocktail Party, 53–54
Carnival Cruise Line, 83
CARONIA, 73–74
Casino, 24, 101–105, 136
Children on shipboard, 27, 74, 149
Classes. See Shipboard
Clothing. See Cruisewear
CNN, 14
Comment cards, 149–50
Corlyon, Diane, 99
Corrigan, Douglas, 10
COSTA RIVIERA, 105
Cozumel, 123
Crew, 129–30, 141–44, 170–71
Cruise director, 148–49, 150–51
Cruise guides, 3–4
Cruise Line International Association (CLIA), 3
Cruise ship design, 60–61; balconies, 68–71; as different from liners, 11–13, 16–17
Cruise staff, 17, 27, 56, 148–49
Cruises: affordability of, 19–27; vs crossing, 32; differences in duration of, 28–37; one class, 12
Cruisewear, 48–49, 58; for day, 49–50, 51–52; for evening, 52–57
CRYSTAL HARMONY, 74, 108, 142

CRYSTAL SYMPHONY, 46–47
Cunard Line, 157
Customs, U.S., 171–72

Dahl, Dr. Eilif, 162
Dancing, 105–107
Departure (sail away), 152–54
Dimenhydrinate, 161
Dining, 79–93, 127; alternative, 89–91; room stewards, 86–89, 132–33, 136, 137–38; saloon, 76–77, 80
Dinner jacket (black tie), 53, 55–57
Disembarkation (final), 95, 170–73
Disney Cruise Line, 87
Dixie Clipper. See Pan Am Clipper
Docking, 112–13; port, 114–15
Dramamine, 161
Dress codes: casual, 53; formal, 53–58; informal, 53; on QUEEN ELIZABETH 2, 52–53

Embarkation, 62–63
Extra-tariff restaurants, 90–91
Entertainment, 98–101

FAIRSEA, 85
Fellini, Federico, 16
Fielding's Guide, 4
First Sitting. See Main Sitting
"Floating hotels," 13
Flying boats, 9, 10
Food, 21–23, 24, 85–86, 88, 93, 117
Formal night, 53–58
FRANCE, 4, 143–44
Freeport (Bahamas), 30

Gilbert & Sullivan, 127
GRAND PRINCESS, 23, 90, 117, 118, 147
Gran Teatro la Fenice, 107
Guthrie, Tyrone, 5

Hakodate (Japan), 124–26
Havana (Cuba), 30–31
HMS Pinafore, 127
Holland America Line, 98, 140, 155
Hope, Bob, 132–33
Horizon Court (GRAND PRINCESS), 90
Hurricane Gloria, 21, 164

ILE DE FRANCE, 11
IMPERATOR, **78, 157**
Immigration, 171–72
In the Mood, 105
ISLAND PRINCESS, 5, 6

James, William, 162

Kolltveit, Bard, 114
Kusadasi (Turkey), 117, 118

LACONIA, 47–48
La Guardia Marine Terminal, 9
Late (second) Sitting, 81, 96–97
Laundry and dry cleaning, 23, 132
LEGEND OF THE SEAS, 4
LEVIATHAN, 11
Lido restaurant, 89–90
Lifeboat drill, 74–75, 95
Lindbergh, Charles, 10
Luggage, 39–48; at customs, 171–72; disembarking, 170, 172; lost, 46–47, 173; off-loading, 129–30

Mail, 10–11; on board, 67
Main (first) Sitting, 81, 96–97
Maître d'hôtel, 79–83, 86, 133, 134, 136–37, 139, 143
MAJESTY OF THE SEAS, **103**

Mann, Derek, 48
MARDI GRAS, **123**
MAURETANIA, 24
Medical center, 23
MERCURY, **78**
Miller, Glen, 105
MONARCH OF THE SEAS, 99, 103, 174
Music, 105–106, 156

Nassau (Bahamas), 29–31
Newpax, 21, 26, 32, 36, 37, 43, 53, 54, 73, 140; description of, 2–3
Newport News, 132
New York Times, The, 14
NIEUW AMSTERDAM, **107**
Nonpax, 6, 7, 15, 18, 21, 26, 29, 30, 31, 36, 37, 46, 48, 49, 136, 144, 152, 161, 174; description of, 2–3
NORDIC PRINCE, **125**
NORDLYS, 4
NORWAY, 4, 55, 63–64, 106
Norwegian Cruise Line, 30
NORWEGIAN DREAM, **84**
NORWEGIAN SEA, **15**
NORWEGIAN SKY, **113**

Ocean liner, 10; as opposed to cruise ship, 11–13, 16–17
Oldpax, 26, 32, 42–43, 73; description of, 1–3
Open sitting, 91–92
ORMONDE, **125**
Out island, 30

PACIFIC PRINCESS, 147
Packing tips, 47–49
Painted Desert (GRAND PRINCESS), 90
Panama Canal, 62
Pan Am Clipper, 9–10, 11
Pan American, 9, 10
Pax, 1, 7
Photographs, 23, 57–58, 62
Pitching (motion), 163–64
Pompeii, 116
Port days, vs sea days, 31–37
Port Said, 116
Pre (and post) cruise packages, 115–16
Promenade decks, 70–71
Promethazine, 161

QUEEN ELIZABETH, 134
QUEEN ELIZABETH 2, 4, 21, **44**, **52**, 52–53, 134, 156, 164
QUEEN MARY, 42
QUEEN MARY 2 (Project), 157
QUEENS GRILL (QUEEN ELIZABETH 2), 21

Railway Express, 42
Reed's Hotel (Funchal), 117
REGAL PRINCESS, **57**
REMBRANDT, 132
Renaissance Cruises, 139
Ritz Hotel, 13, 45
RMS (Royal Mail Ship), 10
Rolling (motion), 164
ROTTERDAM, 5, 28, **54**, 121–22, 132
Royal Caribbean International, 134, 137, 150, 157
ROYAL PRINCESS, 97
Royal Viking Line, 7, 23, 56, 80, 122–23, 137–38
ROYAL VIKING SEA, 19–20, **121**, 138
ROYAL VIKING SKY, **61**
ROYAL VIKING STAR, 104
Rushen, Captain Malcolm, **146**, 147

Saba Island, 174
Sabatini's (GRAND PRINCESS), 90

SAGAFJORD, 141
St. George's (Bermuda), 112, 113
St. Thomas (U.S. Virgin Islands), 120, 124
Salon and spa services, 23, 53, 158
Scapolamine patches, 161
Scending (motion), 165
Seabourn Cruise Line, 91, 139, 140
SEABOURN PRIDE, 26
Sea days, vs port days, 31–37
Sea Goddess, 4, 91, 139
Seasickness, 160–66
Second Sitting. See Late Sitting
Seven-day Caribbean cruise, 31–37
Shipboard: account, 24, 130–31; classes on, 12, 71–73; ethos, 13–18; rituals of, 32–34
Shipmates, 14
Shopping: ashore, 29, 120–22; on board, 24, 50–51, 157
Shore excursions (shorex), 24, 32, 115–20
Show lounge, 97–101
SilverSea Cruises, 55, 91, 139, 140
SKY PRINCESS, 119
SKYWARD, **123**
Slater, Shirley, 4
Social hosts, 106
Sommelier, 86–87
Stabilizers, 164
Steamer trunk, 39–41
Steward(ess), 67–68, 170; cabin, 131–32, 136; dining room, 86–89, 132–33, 136, 137–38
Suitcases, 43–48, 171–72
SUN PRINCESS, 145, 147
STELLA POLARIS, 64

Table selection, 79–85
Tendering port, 114–15
Three and four day cruises, 29–31, 37
Tips, 24, 133–40; to longshoremen, 46; "no tipping" policy, 91–92; "tipping not required, " 140
Thrusters (bow and stern), 112, 124
Transatlantic passage, 11–12
Truffaut, Francois, 169–70
Turnaround, 31; day, 129–33

United States Immigration Service, 12
Unpacking, 22, 73–74
U.S. Customs and Immigration, 171–72

VEENDAM, 102
Venice, 107–108
Verandah Grill (Queen Mary), 90
VOYAGER OF THE SEAS, 157

Wadham, Alan, 145–47, **146**
Wadham, Diane (Parker), 145–47, **146**
Waiters. See Dining room stewards
Ward, Doug, 4
Wardrobe trunks, 41–42
Winchester Cathedral (Southampton), 116
World cruise, 28–29, 55, 73–74, 106; luggage on, 42–43, 46–47; tips, 135
Yeomans, Captain Tony, 97